AUDITORY PROCESSES

Pamela Gillet

Academic Therapy Publications
20 Commercial Boulevard
Novato, California 94949-6191

International Standard Book Number: 0-87879-094-2-R

3 2 1 0 9 8 7
2 1 0 9 8 7 6 5 4

Contents

CHAPTER 1

Auditory Processes

Introduction

Auditory skills include the ability to attend to various sounds, to remember them, to be aware of the direction from which the sound originates, to repeat the sound, to recall sounds, to be aware of sounds in the environment, to be aware of rhythmic patterns, to isolate a sound from a variety of different sounds, to distinguish embedded sounds from background noises, to draw meaning from verbal stimuli, to fuse the sounds coming into two ears into one unified impression, and to identify a sound in the initial, middle, or ending position of a word. The auditory channel functions to keep an individual in contact with the environment at all times. It is the main mode of learning in early childhood. Through the auditory channel, language develops and matures, and shows a meaningful relation to learning and social acceptance.

The auditory modality is of prime importance in the school environment, especially in reading, language development and comprehension, communication, and in the general learning process, i.e., the acquisition and processing of incoming information. The components of the auditory modality encompass auditory acuity, alertness, discrimination, memory, sequencing, figure-ground, and the ability to relate sound-symbol relationships. In the school situation, as well as the everyday world, the child must respond to auditory stimuli, organize them, and understand their meaning.

It is difficult, if not impossible, to separate auditory learning and behavior from other aspects of development. Auditory responses are related to visual perception, motor learning, emotional status, basic intellectual capacity, and the child's experiential background. The development of some basal level of auditory processing would appear to be related to normal language acquisition, school readiness, the reading process, interpersonal relationships, vocational success, and other academic achievement. Particularly important are processes of recognition, identification, localization, discrimination, sequencing of sounds, analysis and synthesis of words, as well as short- and long-term memory. Auditory stimuli place the most significant demands on attention since they are temporally ordered. There is limited opportunity for the listener to review auditory material as is possible with visual material.

Symptomatic behavior of problems in the auditory processing area may be:

— confusion in sounds/words heard
— difficulty in spelling words that are dictated
— problem remembering names and places that are heard
— requests a speaker to repeat what is said on a frequent basis
— difficulty in following directions that have been given orally
— easily distractible by extraneous sounds
— leaves out words and letters when asked to repeat sentences and words
— misinterprets one sound or word for another
— confuses the sequence of sounds, words, and steps in a task when presented verbally
— trouble differentiating one sound from another
— easily distracted by noises
— inability to select and attend to relevant auditory stimuli
— difficulty recognizing a word when only parts are given
— slowness to respond to questions presented orally
— inappropriate responses to relatively simple, age appropriate questions
— inability to gain meaning or the complete meaning from material presented orally

The typical school environment places a heavy emphasis on learning through the auditory modality, especially as the child progresses to higher grades and the emphasis turns to lectures, class discussions, multi-step verbal directions, adult initiated questions, and an increase in the rate of adult-child communication. The student must have sustained listening ability for a variety of auditory stimuli, during a specific time period, and for a series of sequentially formulated directions. Attention must be paid to the teacher's voice with competing background noises such as other voices, shuffling feet, hall noise, etc. Memory for verbally presented rules, a series of directions, and class discussions are a must, especially as the grade levels progress. New auditory signals need to be learned throughout the school experience—e.g., bell systems, PA announcements.

Although reading is primarily visual, acquisition does depend on the auditory processes as well, such as the ability to distinguish similarities and differences in sounds, to perceive a sound within a word, to synthesize sounds into words, and to divide words into syllables. Initially, the reading process involves superimposing the print symbol on the auditory signal, i.e., associating a spoken word with a sequence of printed letters. The phonetic approach to reading may present difficulty for the child determined by the severity of the auditory problems and the number of auditory areas affected. The child may see similarities in words, but does not relate them to their auditory counterparts. He may have difficulty relating part of a word to a whole. Gates noted that "other things being equal, the more familiar the child is with the sound characteristics of words and the more skillful he is in identifying and blending the sound units of the words, the better he is equipped to utilize the phonetic techniques." [1]

The child with auditory problems may be affected in the area of reading in the following ways: (a) difficulty in hearing the similarities in initial and final sounds in words; (b) difficulty in hearing double sounds of consonant blends; (c) difficulty in the discrimination of the short vowel sounds; (d) difficulty in rhyming; (e) difficulty in breaking a word into syllables or individual sounds; (f) difficulty in retaining each of the sounds or syllables; (g) difficulty in blending sounds together as a whole, even though the individual sounds are known; (h) difficulty in

---

[1] A. Gates, *The Improvement of Reading* (NY: MacMillan, 1947): 231.

remembering the sound of a letter or how to say a word, even though the meaning may be known; (i) difficulty in precisely relating the auditory symbol with the visual symbol; (j) may substitute words when reading aloud; (k) may distort the pronunciation of multisyllable words since there is difficulty in sequencing sounds. Auditory problems are also often identified in a child's written work.

A child with an auditory processing problem may not be significantly adversely affected in the area of mathematics depending on the content and the specific approach used in teaching. The auditory processes do, however, impact mathematics learning. In mathematics, the child cannot recall the names of numerals, retain an auditory sequence of numbers, recite multiplication tables, or remember the steps to complete a math operation. In general, the student is unable to follow oral directions, remember verbal instructions, and write down adequate notes from a lecture. The child may have difficulty understanding the words used to describe certain arithmetic processes, especially if visual cues and/or manipulatives are not used. Grasping the word meanings in reasoning problems may be problematic. Numerical symbols, however, appear not to have the corresponding difficulty for this child as verbal symbols.

Although the child's hearing on audiology tests measures well within acceptable limits and the information received by the ear is transmitted to the brain, it may not be structured, recognized, coded, nor stored in the normal manner. For some reason, the brain process necessary for making sense of auditory stimuli may not function in the ordinary way. The child may only be able to attend and react to short units of language. Instructions and directions for this child have to be shortened, simplified, and repeated because he cannot process many units of language fast enough to keep up with the class. Auditory discrimination, in addition, may be poor. This means that the child may hear speech sounds inaccurately. Often this leads to word confusion, particularly if the sounds are similar, e.g., *ladder* for *letter*. Trying to work in a room with activity and background noise is almost impossible for a child who cannot stop himself from attending to all the competing sounds.

The child with a severe auditory problem is unable to structure his auditory world because he has difficulty in sorting out and/or associating sounds with particular objects or experiences.

This child may react to the auditory stimuli by ignoring them as if he did not hear the sounds; or he may respond to each sound as a new experience requiring investigation and attention. In the latter case, he appears to be very hyperactive, exhibiting a short attention span and attending to every sound around him. If attention is not focused on these identified auditory processing disabilities by the team developing the special education student's IEP or by building-based teams and the student's standard education teachers for those who are not receiving specialized programming, it is likely that the vocational and social abilities of these students as they become secondary-aged students will be handicapped in subtle ways by these auditory processing problems.

Auditory processing problems can be ongoing or newly identified. Even with identification and remediation, some students' auditory performance improves as they grow older, but still remains at a lower level than what would be expected for the student's age and level of cognitive functioning. For others, whose educational history shows auditory processing within the expected levels, some aspects of their identified learning disability may have prevented the projected developmental improvements as they grew older. Attention difficulties play a very important role in the current and future auditory performance of students of all ages.

Evaluating the child's auditory processing ability should involve: an assessment of how the child responds to stimuli (location of the sound, discrimination of like and different sounds, quantity of sounds as well as a differentiation of essential sounds from the background); how the stimuli are organized (the sequence, familiarity of the sound, relationship of the sound to other sounds); and the understanding of the meaning of the sounds (classification, memory, analysis). *A Screening Test for Auditory Processing Disorders, The Screening Test of Auditory Perception* (STAP), and the *Screening Test of Adolescent Language* can be used in the screening process when a student who is suspect of having an auditory processing problem is referred for a comprehensive evaluation. If a comprehensive evaluation is determined to be necessary, specific diagnostic tests that measure discrimination, memory, analysis, figure-ground, and synthesis as described in the various sections of this book would be used to validate the existence and determine the intensity of the particular auditory processing problem. In addition to formal testing, informal assessment and clinical observation in the classroom setting can be used to supplement the findings of the formal testing. A comprehensive evaluation must also include an assessment of the student's learning environment and parental information. One test may measure more than one auditory process. Few tests measure all aspects of auditory processing. The outcome of the evaluation should assist the teacher in defining the objectives for instruction.

How the student receives, discriminates, remembers, organizes, and utilizes all the auditory stimuli in the immediate learning, social, and vocational environment will directly influence the level of language, reading, and generalized learning that can be achieved. This is why remediation activities in the auditory processing area are so important. Specific activities need to be included in the curriculum for the development of the auditory processes. Training children in the auditory processes helps them to learn to listen carefully to directions, auditory environmental cues, and details of sounds. The auditory attention span may also be lengthened through appropriate instruction.

When performing auditory training, it is important to always speak directly to the children. Face them when you speak, rather than turning your back to them as you write on the board, turning sideways when giving direction, or subduing your voice while looking down at a paper or book. Sometimes a gentle touch may be used to give the child the physical contact that would bring his attention to the auditory stimuli. Children with auditory processing difficulties always do better if they can both see and hear. Therefore, preferential seating is important in the classroom design as well as the use of visual materials to support the auditory information during the instructional and review process.

The *Language Master* or other equivalent machine can be used to a great advantage with many of the exercises in this booklet. This machine will aid the individualization of remediation. The prepared materials (teacher made or commercial) allow the student to see and hear the sounds, words, phrases, or sentences. He can then respond and make his own voice recording of what he has heard. Finally, he can compare his response with the original stimulus. A tape recorder is also an invaluable aid in an auditory program. Lessons may be developed for individuals or small groups. There are also many excellent auditory tapes in which the child responds either with the recorded voice or immediately after.

The following suggestions were combined from a variety of sources; others are entirely original. They may be used by special education teachers as well as regular classroom teachers who have children with auditory disorders in their classrooms. These activities may be performed by the entire class, in small groups, or individually. They are designed so that they can be integrated into the child's classroom activities without the use of specialized instructional materials.

In all the training activities given in this booklet, auditory and/or visual cues and aids should be given only in the beginning phases and then eliminated as the child becomes more proficient. The best results are seen where these skills are reinforced by regular sessions over a period of time and are consistently incorporated into the reading and language arts program. The focus of any of the exercises presented is not upon the improvement of an isolated skill but rather on improving the behavior that is causing the student difficulty in the learning environment. The activities selected should be the ones that are most similar to those in which the problem exists. For younger children, whenever the exercise calls for teacher action, a puppet may assume that role. Variations in many of the exercises presented may be generated by changing the complexity of the activity and/or by requiring a variety of responses by the student to the task.

The suggestions presented here might stimulate thoughts regarding some of the hows and whys involved in auditory learning and how it can be more consciously and effectively taught. They are all presented with the intent to enhance auditory learning of many different kinds of children. These activities can be used in the special education program as well as for students with auditory processing disorders who are placed within the standard education class. Benefits for everyone may be provided.

Sequencing of Auditory Skill Development Activity

1. Developing an awareness and a responsiveness to the sounds within the child's environment.
2. Imitating sounds—particularly speech sounds.

11

3. Using sounds to communicate. Responses to simple requests.

4. Using words to communicate. Responses to simple requests.

5. Using words of position relative to the child: words that label (using appropriate names or labels for common objects), words of action, words that describe.

6. Responding intelligently to simple questions and simple directions.

7. Speaking in complete sentences rather than incomplete sentences or short phrases.

8. Memorizing jingles, songs, rhymes, poems, etc.

9. Play acting using different voices.

10. Retelling a story. (Read a short four- or five-sentence story. Have the child retell the story, avoiding the use of pronouns.)

11. Relating happenings in sequence.

12. Making up a story and retelling it.

13. Expressing more than one idea in a sentence.

14. Explaining things in a logical, orderly manner.

15. Developing a sense of tonality.

16. Developing a sense of rhythm.

17. Developing awareness of rhythm:
   respond to rhythm with body movement.
   respond to rhythms with musical instruments.
   (As the skill is developed, provide opportunities for reproducing simple rhythms. Gradually vary these rhythms and increase their complexity.)

18. Developing awareness of spoken words as units of speech. ("Dondodat!"—"Don't do that!")

19. Developing an understanding of concepts of direction, time, distance, space, size, rate, etc. (This is best done in conjunction with or following motor patterning.)

20. Utilizing activities involving receiving and following verbal directions of varying number and complexity.

21. Developing a clear understanding of the meanings of words and their relationships to one another.

22. Discriminating the position of sounds in words.

23. Rote learning of phonics either through drill or game type activities. Introduce this activity when the child has demonstrated the ability to write the letters accurately when dictated randomly. Introduce the letter sound in conjunction with the letter configuration, a familiar picture and a word whose meaning is familiar to the child.
24. Using a method of word study whose primary objective is to develop an association between the letter sound and the letter configuration.
25. Studying word families.
26. Syllabification.
27. Systematically studying and applying phonetic and structural analysis.
28. Providing opportunities for creative writing that encourage the child to write as he speaks (either through dictation by the student of his experience stories or student composed and written sentences).*

Suggestions for Helping Students with Auditory Processing Problems in the Regular Education Classroom

1. Provide a printed list of vocabulary words to be used in the lecture/class discussion.
2. Give the student an outline of the material to be presented during the lecture.
3. Present the directions given orally in written or pictorial format.
4. Present short, single focused directions.
5. Use less descriptive, straight forward sentence structure when presenting directions.
6. Write assignments on the board or in the student's notebook or work folder.

---

* From: McLeod, P. *The Undeveloped Learner* (Springfield, Illinois: Charles C Thomas Publisher, 1968).

7. Develop a "buddy system" to check on the assignments and other instructions.

8. Give preferential seating to the student depending on the focus of the auditory presentation.

9. Use filmstrips and captioned films.

10. Use peer tutors to conduct pre-teaching of planned vocabulary and language topics.

11. Gain the student's attention before giving directions or initiating class instruction by a physical touch, cue word, or calling his name.

12. Orient the student to the topic to be presented.

13. Use body language, facial expressions, and gestures.

14. Pace the presentation with occasional pauses between meaningful units to permit time for comprehension.

15. Seat students away from potentially distracting sounds (ventilating fan, door, etc.).

16. Provide short intensive periods of instruction with periods for nonverbal activity and body movement.

17. Permit the student to move to a quiet area when doing silent reading and independent seatwork.

18. Check comprehension of verbally presented material by asking questions related to the material to monitor the student's following and understanding of the material presented.

19. Encourage the students to ask questions when they do not understand what has been said.

20. Rephrase the material since certain words used may have contained sounds and blends that are not easily discriminated.

21. Encourage participation in choral reading, story telling, puppetry, creative dramatics, and informal discussions.

22. Give the directions just before the activity.

23. Provide demonstration.

24. Divide complicated directions into parts; no more than three steps at one time.

25. Provide written directions and cues along with oral lessons.

26. Use an overhead projector to outline points being made in classroom presentations.

27. Shorten sentences when speaking to the students.
28. Use simulation and hands-on learning experiences.
29. Pose a few questions for students to consider as they listen.
30. Wait for class to become quiet before giving directions.
31. Play "follow direction" games.
32. Use less complex vocabulary which is still age appropriate.
33. Use pictures or objects along with verbal comments/ explanations.
34. Wait for a response, sometimes beyond what might be considered to be a normal response time.
35. Use consistent, simple vocabulary to describe tasks.
36. Use associational events to help teach students to retain verbally presented information.

CHAPTER 2

Auditory Discrimination

Introduction

Auditory discrimination is the ability to distinguish similarities and differences in sounds. To identify sounds and words correctly, a child must be able to tell whether sounds or words are the same or different. Before a student can respond appropriately, he/she must be able to perceive the unique qualities of a stimuli and differentiate one stimulus from another. He must be able to tell in which part of the word he hears a particular sound; the initial, medial, or final position. Discrimination of isolated sounds is important, but the child needs to discriminate environmental sounds and qualities of the voice that reflect emotions as well. If the child discriminates incorrectly, he may attach the incorrect meaning to the printed symbols as he reads. Inadequate auditory discrimination skills may result in defective articulation. Auditory discrimination is necessary for learning the phonemic structure of oral language. There can also be degrees of an auditory discrimination problem. A child may be able to distinguish gross but not fine differences.

Auditory discrimination does not relate to the child's understanding of or the ability to give meaning to auditory stimuli. That is a higher level process that will be discussed in the section "Auditory Perception."

Auditory discrimination for word sounds can be weak and faulty in children whose hearing, as measured by acuity tests, is within the normal range. It is not a matter of sensory acuity, but rather one of hearing selectively the beginning, middle, or ending of the word and comparing it with the sound of the corresponding parts of other words, thus having the basis for comparisons and recognition of both similarities and differences. As shown in research studies, the order of increasing difficulties for children in the auditory discrimination area was found to be initial consonant sounds, final consonant sounds, long vowel sounds, and short vowel sounds.

The child with an auditory discrimination problem may be unable to tell the difference in sounds that are alike and different. He may be able to distinguish gross but not fine differences. Difficulty may occur in distinguishing similar parts of words, such as the beginning, middle, or final sounds. He may confuse the meanings of similar sounding words like *cup, cat, cap.* The child may also exhibit articulation disorders in his speech. He might be seen watching the speaker's mouth, in order to lip read. Auditory discrimination skills are necessary for the acquisition of word attack skills in reading.

The phonics approach to reading and spelling is generally difficult for him. If a child incorrectly discriminates the sound he hears, he may attach the wrong meaning to the printed symbols he will try to read. Some children will fail to distinguish the printed symbols *b* and *d* because their auditory equivalents are not distinguished. This confusion of letters can occur on an auditory as well as visual basis. Some children may never learn to discriminate between short vowel sounds, between syllables containing short vowel sounds, or words containing them. These children will need to have special emphasis on learning words through the visual channel. However, even if this child is taught primarily through the visual channel, he is still at a disadvantage, since poor auditory discrimination distorts the receptive, spoken language on which certain skills such as reading, writing, and spelling are based. Often times, a kinesthetic-tactual method supplements other remedial approaches.

The child having problems in the auditory discrimination area is often unable to listen to a word, then supply two or three other words that begin or end with the same sound. Therefore, he is often insensitive to rhymes and cannot pick out words that rhyme or supply words to rhyme with a given word. This ability is fundamental to the construction of "word families" in reading. Auditory discrimination is important in the sound blending areas as well. The child should be able to listen to the pronunciation of a word, sound by sound, and fuse or blend the sounds mentally so as to be able to recognize the word intended.

Poor auditory discrimination skills may be the result of living in impoverished environments where loud background noises interfere with the ability of the child to distinguish speech sounds. The limitation of verbal stimuli found in these families adds to the auditory deficiency. Having learned a dialect or another language appears to lessen the child's auditory discrimination abilities with the English language sounds.

Activities used to develop auditory discrimination involve accurate listening and attention to sounds; listening for likenesses and differences in sounds, spoken words, and letters; becoming aware of rhyming patterns in spoken words; comparing sounds in pitch, loudness, direction, and distance; discriminating these distinctions against background sounds; recognizing specific sounds; and identifying the source of sounds. The remedial technique must be multisensory, combining sound with other stimuli.

Initially, auditory discrimination activities should use only sounds and words with which the child is familiar. Auditory discrimination activities should involve listening for gross sounds, isolated consonant sounds, initial sounds in words, final sounds, and short and long vowel sounds. When dealing with consonant sounds, it is helpful to begin with sounds that can be sustained such as *s, m, n, f, sh,* and *v.* For training in initial sounds, the words presented should begin with sounds that are auditorally different. Teaching similar sounding words requires a high degree of auditory discrimination that certain children may not have. Gradually, words should be presented that begin with sounds that are more closely alike. Words beginning with blends such as *sn, sk, st, sl,* and *sp* should be avoided in the initial stages of listening for beginning sounds. After mastering discrimination of beginning and final sounds, the children can be asked to listen for specific sounds and indicate whether that sound comes at the beginning or the ending of a word. In the vowel sounds, it is suggested that after listening to long vowels in isolation, the exercises proceed to the short vowel sounds in isolation rather than having the child listen to vowel sounds within words.

In developing auditory discrimination, a variety of devices can be used. In general, the technique is to provide a list of spoken words containing the element to be taught, allow the children to focus attention on the particular sounds in the words, allow them to compare words which contain the sound with words which do not. For example, in teaching *f* as an initial consonant, some of the usable techniques are:

1. Ask the children to listen to a list of words and tell you how they are alike. Pronounce such words as *fun, fox, field, fairy, fat, Fred.* Ask how they are alike. Then pronounce each word again while printing it on the chalkboard. Explain that all the words begin with the letter *f* which has the sound *fff.* Underline the *f* in each word as you pronounce it again. Let one child at a time point to the *f* as you pronounce the word a third time.

2. Play a listening game in which the children signal, by raising a hand, clapping, or standing, whenever you pronounce a word which begins with *f.* Use lists such as *fit, fan, make, frog, fence, toy, fireplace, Friday,* and so on. Then reverse by having them signal when they do not hear a word beginning with *f* using lists in which about half of the words do not begin with *f.*

3. Ask the children to suggest other words which begin with *f.* To make this more challenging, it may be done by categories, i.e., names, animals, objects, or games to play. If desired, the words can be put on the board and the *f*s underlined.

4. Give incomplete sentences or riddles which the children are to finish by adding a word which begins with *f.* For example:
   Playing ball is lots of *(fun).*
   My cat has nice soft *(fur).*
   What game do boys like to play in the fall? *(football)*
   What do birds do in the air? *(fly)*

5. After two or more sounds have been taught, practice should be given in discriminating among them. One way of doing this is to pronounce a mixed list of words and have the children either say or write the specific sound and letter they were to listen for.[1]

---

[1] Albert Harris, *How to Increase Reading Ability* (New York: David McKay, 1970).

The teacher should aim to improve auditory discrimination abilities by the method which succeeds best with the child. Try teaching:

Only auditory—have the child close his eyes so vision does not disturb auditory discrimination.

By the intensification of auditory stimulus—make the sounds louder, being sure background noise is at a reduced level.

By visual cues—show the child the visual representation of the auditory stimulus; show the child how the sound is made on the lips, position of the tongue and teeth, etc.

Kinesthetically—have the child touch his own or the teacher's voice parts. Watching the teacher's lips, feeling his and the teacher's voice parts as they work, and looking at his own production of speech sounds in a mirror may be beneficial in the earlier remedial training.

After the child has shown success in responding verbally or through gesture or manual expression to the auditory discrimination exercises, paper-and-pencil exercises can be initiated.

Tests that may be used in evaluating the auditory discrimination area are:

Wepman Auditory Discrimination Test
Boston University *Speech Sound Picture Discrimination Test*
Monroe Reading Aptitude Test
Seashore Measures of Musical Talents (rhythm subtest)
Steck-Vaughn Reading Readiness Test
SCAN (filtered word subtest)
Valett's *Developmental Survey of Basic Learning Abilities* (auditory discrimination subtest)
TOLD-Primary
SRA Achievement Series (language perception subtest)
Doren Diagnostic Reading Test of Word Recognition Skills (rhyming subtest)
Gates-MacGinitie Reading Tests
Harrison-Stroud Reading Readiness Profiles
Murphy-Durrell Reading Readiness Analysis (phoneme subtest)
Stanford Diagnostic Reading Test (auditory discrimination subtest)

Diagnostic Reading Test of Word Analysis Skills I and II
Goldman, Fristoe, and Woodcock Diagnostic Auditory Discrimination Test
Standard Reading Test
Robbins Speech Sound Discrimination and Verbal Imagery Type Test
Test of Nonverbal Auditory Discrimination
Macmillan Reading Readiness Test, Revised
Kindergarten Evaluation of Learning Potential
Ann Arbor Learning Inventory
SCREEN: Senf-Comrey Ratings of Extra Educational Need (auditory skills subtest)
American School Reading Readiness Test, Revised
Accelerated Speed Perception Test
Flowers Auditory Test of Selective Attention
Screening Test for Auditory Perception
Test of Awareness of Language Segments (TALS)
Lindamood Auditory Conceptualization Test, Revised (LAC)
Nemner Group Test of Auditory Discrimination
Kindergarten Auditory Screening Test
Screening Test for Identifying Children with Specific Language Disabilities

Remedial Exercises

1. The teacher places several rhythm instruments before the child and demonstrates the sound of each. The child is asked to turn his back and listen while the teacher makes noises with one of the instruments. Then the child is asked to duplicate the sound that he heard. This may be done by asking the child to select a picture of "what is making the sound." The child might also be asked to say words that best describe each sound he heard.

2. Place the following objects in four identical glass jars: wooden beads, glass beads, pebbles, and a spoon. The child is to watch as the teacher demonstrates the sound of each. The child turns his back and listens, and then tries to duplicate the sound he heard.

3. Make Montessori sound boxes from eight milk cartons. Fill pairs with the following: two teaspoons corn, two

teaspoons rice, two teaspoons sugar, two pennies. Cover four of one set in one fabric and four of the other set in another fabric. Ask the child to match up the boxes with the same sounds. Slowly diminish the contrast and increase the number of pairs as the year progresses.

4. Tell the child he is to clap whenever he hears a sound *f*. Utilizing both visual and auditory cues, have him perform several sample exercises. Explain now that you're going to try to fool him by mixing his sound with others, i.e., *b*, *m*, *f*, *s*, *th*, etc. When trying to fool him, the teacher should place a white card before her mouth to limit visual cues.

5. The teacher may ask a child to tell if the following words are the same or different:

rug-bug	cap-nap	boy-bay
fan-van	hat-rat	foo-loo

For the child who reads, a worksheet is prepared with rows of words similar in sound. The teacher reads a word, the child circles the word he hears (auditory-visual association).

6. Ask the child to put "thumbs up" whenever he hears the sound which has been previously introduced. This may be done when listening to simple poems or sentences.

7. The teacher may ask the child to tell her the two words that begin with the same sound: *cow, boat, ladder, bell*. This activity may be simplified by asking if two words start with the same sound.

8. Blindfold the child. Can he discriminate sound by the matching of noisemakers (bells, horns, drum, etc.) with the sound each makes?

9. Tape record voices of friends and have the child identify the voices. This might be done for the greeting exercise in the morning.

10. The children form a circle with one child blindfolded in the middle. They say, "We are now circling and having fun. But now one will speak. Can you guess the right one?" The child in the center guesses; the child who spoke takes his place.

11. Dramatize the sound such as *s* (the kettle boiling) or *t* (the clock ticking).

12. Talk about "what things say": the "drip-drop" of a water faucet; the train wheels go "clickety-clack."

13. The child is shown an object accompanied by sound. He later covers his eyes while the sound is made. The child points to the object making the sound. (Examples of environmental sounds: wall switch on and off, door opened and shut, handbag clasp opened and shut, alarm clock winding and ringing, scraping of chair on floor, pouring of water, rattling of keys, crumpling or tearing paper, etc.) Later, have the child discriminate these sounds with slight background noise: drums, taps, bells, rhythm sticks, tone blocks, rattles, triangles, etc.

14. Select a story or poem in which some sound, element, blend, or word appears frequently. For example, the long *o*, the *pl* blend, or the word *and*. Be sure that the children understand what they are to listen for; then read the selection. Have them clap once every time they hear the sound or have them count the number of times, etc. When the children appear to have performed well on the selection, try adding a variety of responses. For example, on hearing the long *o*, they must clap once, but on hearing the word *and*, they must snap their fingers once. This exercise can be made more difficult by adding distracting background noises.

15. The teacher reads orally a silly sentence, for example, "Sally smiles sweetly at Sue." Which word does not begin with the *s* sound? Initially, tell the children what to look for.

16. The teacher gives consonants in pairs: *s-m, s-s, f-n, f-f, n-s.* The children reply by raising their hands if the sounds are alike.

17. Wrap a small gift with many layers of paper. Music plays as the package is passed around the circle. The child who is holding the package when the music stops begins to unwrap it. When the music resumes, the package is passed on again. Repeat.

18. Play children's records which contain a variety of sounds such as fire engines, trains, church bells, animals, clocks, etc. Have the children identify the sounds. All recordings

should be clear and of adequate length to allow the child to distinguish each sound.

19. Teach discrimination of phonetic elements. Begin with consonants, then long vowels, blends, and short vowels. Have the children recognize the *sounds*, not the letter names. For example, say a series of short vowel sounds:

    (1) "a-i-a-o-i-a-a"

    Have the children raise their hands when they hear the *a* sound.

    (2) "a-i"; "o-a"; "a-a";
    later: "hat-hit"; "hat-hat"

    Have the children raise their hands if the pairs are alike in sound.

    (3) "ab-ib-ob-ab" (nonsense)

    Have the children raise their hands when they hear the *ab* sound.

    (4) "ib-ab"; "ab-ab"

    Have the children tell if the pairs are alike, etc. Later use short *e* and short *u* sounds.

20. Teach recognition of rhyming words. Have the children listen to the teacher or a tape recording. Proceed in the manner listed above. Choose words that contain the vowel that you are emphasizing, such as "sack, lick."

21. Additional teaching of phonetic sounds.

    (1) Say several words, "cat, sit, hop, tan." Have the children raise their hands when they hear the *a* sound.

    (2) Say three words, "cat, hop, tan." Have the children identify which two have the same sound.

22. One child says a word, such as "sky." Each child in turn gives a word that rhymes with it until all common words rhyming with it are used up. Another set is started. For example, "dug, bug, chug, jug." Then "hit, mit, fit, sit, bit," etc.

23. Ask the child to say a consonant sound that can be sustained *(m, s, sh, v)*. Tell him to continue using the sound while you say others *(t, b, s, f)*; and ask him to stop the sound as soon as you say the one he is making. Later, tell the child to "think" the sound, but not say it out loud. Then

the teacher says other sounds, asking him to raise his hand when he hears the teacher say the sound he is *thinking*.

24. Have the child listen to lists of words while concentrating on one sound. Have him signal when he hears the sound.

25. Give the child a word and have him give as many words as possible which have the same beginning, middle, or ending sounds.

26. Play games having the children be animals. Have them make sounds like ducks, with the exception of one chicken. Have a child come in from the outside to identify the chicken.

27. Say It-Take It. Put a variety of objects on a table, the names of which contain sounds being studied by the child. Say the sound *p*, for example. The child has 30 seconds to find an object on the table which has the *p* sound in it. After he has found the object, he must repeat the sound given, then name the object. If the child is unable to find the item after 30 seconds, repeat the process or choose another sound.

28. Play listening games in which one child softly taps, rings a bell, claps, or calls to a "listener" who stands in front of the room with his back to the class. The "listener" has three guesses to identify the sound.

29. Say a series of four words, three of which begin with the same letter. Ask which one does not belong. The same can be done with ending sounds. Worksheets may be utilized later.

30. Speak a sentence, pronouncing one word incorrectly. Have the child say the word that is mispronounced, and then pronounce it correctly. (This is good for auditory perception, also.)

31. The teacher should be facing the backs of the children's heads. Call out a list of words and have the students raise their hands if they hear a word *without* the sound they are listening for. (This would have been provided by the teacher before the series of words is read.) This exercise can be used for beginning, middle, and ending sounds. The teacher would merely denote this at the initiation of the exercise, i.e., beginning sound *f*.

32. Put some sounds on the board. The teacher should say the sound. Instructions given to the class are: "Look around the classroom and say all the things you see in the room beginning with the sound." The exercise can be varied to include having the sound in the beginning, middle, or ending position.

33. Ask the child to draw a line between the picture and the sound he hears.

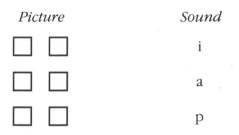

Picture	*Sound*
□ □	i
□ □	a
□ □	p

34. Give the child a list of words and have him underline the word he hears.

35. Ask the child to mark the picture that rhymes with the word you say.

36. Show the child some pictures and ask him to mark the one that does not start with a particular letter.

37. Train Game. A picture of a train is placed in front of the child with an engine, freight car, and caboose. Point out the first, middle, and last cars. The child is given the stimulus sound. He then repeats it. He is then asked to designate whether this sound comes in the initial, medial, or final position in the words said by the teacher by pointing to the proper car in the train.

38. Find the Sound. The teacher shows the child the object making the noise. She demonstrates the sound. She then hides behind objects and asks him to find the object. This may be done by having the child close his eyes and turn towards the direction from which he hears the sound coming.

39. To discriminate loud and soft sounds, a xylophone can be played. Play a note; after a short pause, tell the children you will play the same note; and they will have to say if this note was either softer or louder than the first one.

(This activity is also useful for developing auditory memory.)

40. Ask the children to form a line facing you. Each time the second note is louder than the first, they may all take one step forward. When the second note is softer than the first, they stay in the same place. Those who move forward on a softer note are penalized by taking two steps backward. Those children reaching the front of the room first are winners. (This involves auditory memory, also.)

41. The teacher plays one note on the piano or xylophone and, after a pause, plays other notes slowly. The children raise their hands when the original note is played again. No response is made when other notes are played. (Auditory memory is involved here, also.)

42. The children are to listen to a series of sentences and act out the one that is different. "Touch your arm. Touch your arm. Wave your hand. Touch your arm."

43. When the teacher says the phoneme "f-f-f," the child is expected to lay in a line three squares of the same color. If the teacher says "v-f-m," the child is expected to select three squares of different colors. This same type exercise may be used for initial, medial, and final sounds in words.

44. Echo Game. One child chants a word or sentence; another child across the room echoes it in softer tones. Tapping or clapping in a rhythmic sequence can be employed. (This is useful for auditory memory, also.)

45. The teacher hides a ticking clock. The children must find it with the aid of the ticking sound only.

46. Use cards with symbols and pictures to help teach sounds. Have the child listen for a sound and then select a picture which represents the sound. (This is useful for auditory-visual association.)

47. Have the child sort pictures according to the sounds he hears at the beginning, middle, or end of the words. (This is useful for auditory-visual association.)

48. Make sound booklets, selecting pictures that start or end with particular given sounds. (This is useful for auditory-visual association.)

49. Words can be put on the board or on worksheets. Read the words and ask the class in what way they are alike.

The children are asked to underline the parts that are all alike. This exercise can be followed for all sound positions. (This is useful for auditory-visual association.)

50. Pass blank papers to the children. A typical lesson might be: "I will say a word twice. After I say it twice, I want you to write . . .

    (1) the first sound."
    (2) the long vowel you hear."
    (3) the beginning blend."
    (4) the last sound."
    (5) a rhyming word."

51. Using tin cans and heavy strings, let the children make play telephones. The string is pulled tight, and the children begin transmitting vocal sounds.

52. Say three words to the child, two of which are alike. Have the child select the two that begin the same way. (Middle and final sounds can also be used.)

53. Tape record a series of sets containing two sounds, some of which vary substantially and others of which are alike. Using a prenumbered piece of paper, have the children listen to each sound and place a mark next to the number of each set which sound alike. Gradually, develop a taped inventory of sets of words, musical selections, and sounds which differ on more than one dimension.

54. Use instruments such as a bell, whistle, etc. Play two of them. Ask the child, "Which one did you hear first?" (This is good for auditory memory, also.)

55. In teaching letter sounds, it may be found helpful to identify as many of these sounds as possible with familiar sounds. "What sound do you make when you blow out a candle?" "What sound do you make when you eat something good?"

56. Draw a ball field on tagboard. Each child tries to make a home run by thinking of a word beginning with each of the three letters. If teaching rhyming words, place words around the bases. The child thinks of words rhyming with the words on the bases.

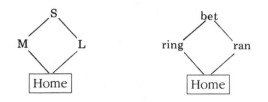

57. Make several large cardboard trains. Each car of the train should have two or more slits for the insertion of word cards. Each player has a train. The leader shows a sound, and if the player can say it, he may place the card in his train. The player whose train is first completely filled with cards wins.

58. One student or the teacher pronounces a word; then, the next student pronounces it and gives another word that begins with the same sound or ends with the sound.

59. Sound Wheels (visual cues). The child spins a circle and reads the words he has made (both wheels rotate).

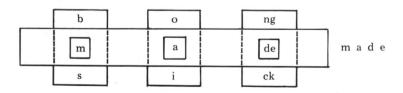

phonograms:
all, and, ang, ent, est.   consonants: *c, d, f, g, h, l,* etc.

Commercial materials of this type are: *PhonoWord Wheels* (Steck), *Webster Word Wheels* (Webster), and *Phonetic Word Analyzer* (Milton Bradley).

60. Phonic Card (visual cues).

b		o		ng
m		a		de	m a d e
s		i		ck

The first strip contains initial consonants; the second strip, middle vowels; and on the third, common word endings. The child moves the strips up and down, and reads the words he has made. This can be adapted for practice on beginnings, middles, and endings of words or using phonograms (sound blending, also).

61. Rhyme Making. Lines of verses are printed on separate strips. The child picks out all the lines ending in the same sound, assembles the poem, and reads it.

62. Dot Game. Ditto masters can be made of "dot pictures," using consonants or blends for each dot. The sounds are pronounced, and the child draws a line for all the dots of the corresponding sound.

63. The child can listen to recorded sounds and then be asked to demonstrate the activity such as opening a door, scraping a chair across an uncarpeted floor, etc.

64. To help in discriminating beginning and final sounds, the teacher can tap on the child's chest when the sounds come at the front of the word and tap on his back if the sound comes at the back of the word. This should be used just until the child has the idea of listening for the beginning and/or ending sound.

65. Ask the child to observe the teacher ring a bell. The child is asked to raise his hand as soon as he hears the bell. When the child has learned this task, he should be asked to perform the same task with his eyes closed. The next step is to have the child raise his hand when he hears the bell and to immediately lower his hand when he no longer hears it. Later, he can identify location of the sound. The teacher can vary the location. The child can also respond by dropping beads in a jar, tapping a table, etc.

66. Mother Cat and Her Kittens. At least five children can play this game. Have one child be "mother cat." The kittens scatter to various parts of the room. Mother cat falls asleep. Then she calls, "Where are my kittens?" Kittens meow and mother identifies location.

67. Sound Detection Game. The children form a circle. "It" in the middle is blindfolded. He points to any child who is supposed to make the sound of an animal. "It" has to guess who is making the sound and what it represents.

68. The Sounding Box. The teacher has a box with objects in it. There are other boxes with the consonant letters that have been studied marked on them. Each child takes an object out of the box, says the name, what letter it begins with, and puts it in the proper letter box. For example, a

pen would go in the "p" box while a button would go in the "b" box.

69. Play a game of musical chairs. Make the volume softer and softer. The children will have to attend more selectively as the pressure and noise of the game increases.

70. Record a portion of the class activities on a tape recorder, but do not identify the children by name. Can they recognize who is talking? Can they recognize the activity taking place? (This can be used for a "circle" activity.)

71. Have the students put their heads down and listen. After a period of listening, have the children tell sounds they heard by:

   (1) matching picture to sounds heard,
   (2) telling what the sound is, and
   (3) describing the sound in detail.

72. A field trip with tape recorder, either a family or class project. Tape zoo sounds, airport sounds, music class, or a concert for playback and listening activities.

73. Pairs. Have pictures of pairs of objects with similar sounding names. Say both names. Then ask the children to put a marker on one of them. For example, say *cat-mat.* Put a bean on *mat. Bat-mat,* put a bean on *bat. Moon-spoon,* put a bean on *spoon. Rake-cake,* mark *rake.* (This is good for visual perception, also.)

74. Sounding Bingo. Each child has a 9" x 12" sheet of tagboard. The letter symbols of the sounds being studied are printed in squares on the tagboard. The arrangement varies with each chart. The teacher holds up a flash card and calls on a child to give the sound. Each child locates the letter on his card and places a marker on it. From here on, the usual bingo arrangements may be used or every card may be filled so that every child is a winner. (This is good for visual perception, also.)

75. Pronounce the words in each group. Listen and tell the position in which the indicated consonant blend is heard in each word.

   st: first, stamp, understood
   th: Catholic, both, those
   sh: fishing, shoes, push

thr: throw, threw, three
tw: twelve, between, twenty
sp: speak, clasp, spend
ch: choose, porch, pitcher
pl: please, explain, plate
str: strange, strong, street
cr: cried, sacred, secret
cl: clown, class, cloth
tr: tricks, country, train

76. When teaching words that have sounds that are alike, color code those sounds that are alike with the same color. (This is useful for auditory-visual association.)

77. On a list of rhyming words, ask the child to circle the parts of the words that are alike. This draws attention to the point that rhyming words have parts that are said and spelled in a similar manner.

78. Written exercises for auditory discrimination can involve "change." Given stimulus words, ask the child to change a vowel to create a new word (C*at*—c*ut*—c*ot*); change the beginning consonant (*l*et—*b*et—*m*et); change the ending consonant (si*t*—si*p*—si*n*).

79. Prepare a set of cards with words having the same phonogram: *fill, hill, bill, mill.* Prepare a poster with a list of riddles. "My word is *fill.* Change one letter and get something we use to grind flour. Change one letter and get something which is part of a bird." The child looks at the set of prepared cards to select the correct word to complete the riddle. After the child has become accustomed to the exercise, cue cards need not be made. (This is good for visual perception, also.)

80. Have the child make up a riddle whose answer begins with the last letter of the answer to the previous riddle. "I say meow . . . *cat.* I am the opposite of bottom . . . *top.* I am a green round vegetable that comes in a pod . . . *pea.*" (This is good for auditory perception, also.)

81. Have index cards prepared with letters, dipthongs, blends, digraphs, etc. When the child hears the sound, he holds up the index card with the appropriate sound.

82. Exercises can be given so that the child signals by clap-

ping, raising his hand, etc., when a nonrhyming word is called.

83. Using pictures or picture cards, have the child find all the pictures that sound like "_____" or sort into groups all the cards that have words that sound alike.

84. Tell the child to listen for a specific sound in a word. Say a word and ask, "Is the sound at the beginning or end of this word?"

85. Read a sentence to the child with a missing word and ask the child to fill in the missing word with a word that rhymes with it. "The bird was sitting on its _____ ." The word I'm looking for rhymes with "vest."

After the children have established a pattern of success with these auditory discrimination exercises, the teacher might want to have a record or tape playing softly in the background while the children are doing a specific listening task. They will be attending to foreground sounds while there is *structured* background noise. (See section on Auditory-Figure Ground.)

CHAPTER 3

Auditory Memory

Introduction

General memory refers to global, gross forms of retaining information. Sequential memory is involved in remembering things presented in a specified order. Memory also refers to the ability to retrieve that information from storage when needed.

Auditory memory involves the ability to retain and recall material presented through the auditory channel. This material does not necessarily involve repetition of pattern or sequence. The degree of auditory memory of a child is generally evaluated by output: oral and written expression as well as the demonstrated ability to follow oral directions.

Meaning is important when talking about auditory memory. The more meaningful the material, the better it is retained. The shorter in length the materials, the easier auditory memory becomes. Complexity of the auditory stimuli should also be considered. The movement in complexity should be from names of concrete, familiar objects to pictures, numbers, letters, words, and finally sentences. When the teacher gives auditory directions or information to a child, she needs to consider the meaningfulness and complexity of the language, as well as the length of the auditory presentation. Therefore, when auditory information is complex, lengthy, and competes with irrelevant stimuli, auditory memory is depressed.

The child with an auditory memory problem may not remember names of people or objects in the class or home environment with which he should be quite familiar. He often does not know rote sequences, i.e., his alphabet, counting sequence, multiplication tables, his address, or phone number. He is unable to remember several directions, or cannot supply a word to a well known poem, greeting, story, or rhyme. He may have more difficulty with nonmeaningful units than meaningful, and with long-term, more than short-term memory. Sometimes there is no difficulty remembering single words but is limited by the amount of information that can be remembered at any one time.

A child with difficulty in this area may be severely handicapped in a variety of ways—in storing information, in reading, in following directions, in initiating words and sentences, and in developing language. Disorders in auditory memory also cause problems in developing a grammatical language structure and appropriate sentence patterns. In fact, all aspects of language are dependent on auditory memory.

In reading new words, auditory memory of letter sounds has to be automatic in recalling the speech sound. To read new words or say these words, the sounds need to be sequenced. Auditory memory problems can lead to faulty comprehension since the child may expend time on trying to remember words or sounds.

A child with auditory memory deficiencies might be given attention clues (visual or auditory) so that he can "be ready to listen," trained in the learning strategy of organizational skills so that he can organize what he must remember in a meaningful way, and be provided the opportunity for reauditorization, to orally repeat the instructions. Presenting words in pairs, in association, in context, and by category facilitates auditory memory in children. Permitting the student to use visual cues and to write as he memorizes are other general remedial techniques. Word associations often help facilitate recall: "bread and butter," "black and white."

Often, poor auditory learning results from an inability to appreciate the sequence of auditory events. Some authors and practitioners in the learning disability field draw a distinct line between exercises for auditory memory and auditory sequencing, since there is a difference between recalling information and recalling information in proper sequence. Auditory sequencing involves the number of patterns that can be recalled from oral stimuli. This includes immediate and delayed recall of digits, words, sentences, events in a story, etc. The child with an auditory sequencing problem often has difficulty in mispronunciation of words (emeny), of compound words (millwind), or phrases (Where they are?). Auditory sequencing problems may be reflected in an inability to learn the days of the week, months of the year, etc. In a series of directions, the first or last is often remembered, but not all those given. Children with auditory memory problems will often be able to remember and carry out instructions if they are given in small units, one at a time with planned silent pauses between the units. Deficits in auditory memory may also cause impairments in auditory blending (see Auditory Synthesis section), causing the child to have trouble recognizing a word when it is broken down into its phonetic components and presented verbally. These children also have problems in reading when comparative word clues are given since the auditory memory problem may make the model or comparative word unavailable for comparison. When auditory memory is impaired, learning from experience is more difficult because the auditory aspects of the experience (what was said) are not well retained.

Auditory memory problems may keep the child from recalling numbers. He recognizes the correct number when it is heard, but he cannot say the one he wants. He may self-monitor and be able to realize he has said a number incorrectly in isolation or during an oral calculation, but does not have the ability to retrieve the correct one. Rapid, oral math drills are very confusing and frustrating for a child with an auditory memory problem. When the steps of an arithmetic process are presented or when a reasoning problem is read orally, the auditory memory deficit will also interfere with the retention of the steps or all the information needed to solve the problem. Oral work should be kept to a minimum and visual back-up must be available.

Activities used to develop auditory sequencing involve recalling a sequence or pattern of gross sounds, the sequenced events in stories, letters of words, the order of compound words or words in sentences, patterns of loudness and rhythm, speech sounds or a sequence of words by verbal or manual reproduction of the initiated pattern. In training in the auditory sequencing area, it is advisable to use content that the child will utilize in everyday life. It is also very important to be sure the teacher has the child's attention before beginning any exercise for remediating this area. It generally helps to wait a few seconds after saying an attention-getting word since a brief moment of quiet before the presentation facilitates listening and recall.

In the remediation process, attention to details in the patterns to be remembered can be accentuated by using motor cues, such as tapping, as each item is given. Teach the child to group elements of a sequence in clusters as large as possible and to visualize the sequence to be remembered whenever possible.

Testing for auditory memory includes the repetition of digits, sounds, words, phrases, and sentences randomly and in sequence. Auditory memory and sequencing can be measured by:

Wechsler Intelligence Tests for Children, Revised
Illinois Test of Psycholinguistic Abilities, Revised (ITPA) (auditory vocal sequencing subtest)
Goldman, Fristoe, and Woodcock Auditory Memory Tests
Schull Sentence Repetition Test
Detroit Tests of Learning Aptitude (auditory attention span for unrelated words subtest, auditory attention span for related syllables and oral commission subtests)
California Short Form Test of Mental Maturity (memory subtest)
Learning Efficiency Test-II
Wide Range Test of Memory and Learning (WRAML)
Clymer-Barret Pre-Reading Battery
Cooperative Primary Tests
Auditory Pointing Test
Auditory Sequential Memory Test
Lindamood Auditory Conceptualization Test, Revised
Language Structured Auditory Retention Span Test
Woodcock-Johnson Psychoeducational Battery (cognitive abilities tests and sentence memory subtests)
Durrell Analysis of Reading Difficulty
Binet (repeating digits and memory for sentence items)
Parsons Language Sample (digit and sentence repetition)
Auditory Memory Span Test
Carrow Auditory-Visual Abilities Test
Brown-Carlsen Listening Comprehension Test
Short-Term Auditory Retrieval and Storage Test
McCarthy Scales of Children's Abilities (verbal memory subtests)

Screening Tests for Identifying Children with Specific Language Disabilities

SCREEN: Senf-Comrey Ratings of Extra Educational Needs (auditory skills subtest)

Ann Arbor Learning Inventory

Screening Test for Auditory Perception (STAP) (remembering rhymes subtest)

Remedial Exercises

1. Rhythm patterns aid auditory memory. Any chants or rhythmic patterns attached to language units can be used as a remedial approach in the beginning stages.

2. The child is asked to point to a specific object in the room and name it. The next child points to and names the first object and then adds his own. The children continue until they are unable to recall the objects and names in correct order.

3. The child is asked to watch and listen as the teacher drops beads into a can. Then the child is asked to drop the same amount into his own can. The activity should be repeated with the child's eyes closed.

4. Have the child listen to chimes on a clock and respond by telling the correct time.

5. Tap out an irregular sequence of three to five taps and have the children imitate the series, i.e., tap-tap-rest-tap-tap. This may be done on a table top or with a percussion instrument.

6. The child may be asked to follow a series of directions, working from the simple to the more complex.

    "Sit in your seat."

    "Put the hat on the doll and put the doll on the floor."

    "Open your spelling book, close the book, put the book on my desk, hop around the room on one foot, and sit down in your seat."

    One command may be given and then added to.

    "Bring me a pencil."

    "Bring me a pencil and a book."

"Bring me a pencil, a book, and then give the book to Sally."

7. The teacher may ask a child to provide the next sound or word from a pattern. The teacher may play a drum, a bell, a bell and a drum, and ask the child for the next musical sound. Or she may say "slish, slash, slish," and ask the child for the next word. After any of these activities, the child should repeat the entire pattern.

8. Place a white card in front of the teacher's mouth to limit visual cues, and ask the child to repeat a series of nonsense syllables ("ba, da, ta"), pitch changes, digits, phrases, and sentences.

9. Have a child repeat a pressed out pattern on the buzzer board. Patterns produced on the piano, with melody bells, and other rhythm instruments can be used effectively here, also.

10. Clap out a simple pattern and then ask one child to repeat it by clapping. The child who can correctly replicate the pattern then creates a new one, and so on, around the class. Variations of this include tapping with a pencil or ruler and the use of rhythm instruments (bells, clappers, sticks). With older children, the use of groups of words related around a central idea can be used. For example, *stove, pot, cook, heat.* Word chains such as these can be increased. Word chains with the beginning same sound may also be used (*bed, bug, bet*).

11. Play a short story on a tape recorder or read it aloud. When the story is finished, ask the child questions about the story. "Who or what was talking in the story?" "What happened to him or it?" "How did the story finish?" "What do you think happened next?" News items are good for this type of exercise since they are short and cover pertinent areas, "who, what, when, where, how, and why."

12. A higher level of auditory memory might involve the teacher spelling a word to the student. Pencils and paper are not used. However, during the newness of the exercise, the children may trace the letters on the tops of their desks or in the air while the teacher spells it. A child may be called upon to say the word and/or write it on the blackboard.

13. Imitation Game. With the pupil's back turned, the teacher bounces a ball three times, snaps fingers, taps the desk with a pencil, coughs, taps a glass with a spoon, etc. The child turns and imitates what he heard. Tape record and compare the original to the child's response.

14. Story Game. The teacher tells a very simple story. First she says, "Listen carefully while I tell this story, because I will ask you a question to see how well you remember it." The teacher begins with a three-sentence story. For example: "Bobo was a happy clown. He wore a suit with large yellow polka dots on it. He liked the circus." Question: "What was on Bobo's suit?" The teacher continues the story asking for details. She makes the story easier or harder, depending on the ability of the children she intends to call on.

15. Remember the Word in the Middle. The teacher says, "Listen carefully while I say some words. The teacher then says three words. For example, *Building, children, school.* Who can remember which word was in the middle?" In the beginning, to make the exercise easier, the end words may rhyme, such as, *fight, see, light.*

16. The teacher says a short rhyme, and the children repeat it. For example, "We have fun, when we run." The children repeat. "I will buy, an apple pie." Again, the children repeat.

17. The Store Game. "Tom's mother sent him to the store. She told him to buy . . . ." The teacher then asks the children who can remember what his mother told him to buy and in the correct order.

18. I Went On A Trip. The children sit in a circle. The first child says, "I went on a trip. In my suitcase I put . . . " and he names one object. The next child repeats the object he named, adds one more, and so on. The objects must be named in the correct order. If a child misses, he is out of the game. This game should be played in small groups. The teacher may vary the size of the group according to the children's ability to remember.

19. SoundsRound About. The children close their eyes and are as quiet as possible. Ask them to listen for and remember all the sounds they can hear inside or outside

the room. After 20 or 30 seconds, the children may report on the clock ticking, someone sneezing, a truck going by, people talking outside, etc. The children may also try to locate the direction of the sounds. (This is useful for auditory discrimination, also.)

20. Story Memory. The teacher reads a very simple story every day for a week without changing it in any way. On Friday, the teacher tells the story, stopping at intervals and calling on various children to fill in the thought.

21. Give the child a list of nonsense syllables. Repeat the list, leaving out one syllable. Have the child identify the one left out. This may be then done with meaningful word units.

22. Have a student recall past happenings and relate these to the group during opening exercises or language circle, i.e., "Tell us about what you did on the weekend." "What did you get for your last birthday?"

23. Have the child listen to a record or the radio each day to obtain specific information, such as baseball scores, the weather, etc. Have him report his findings to the class.

24. Restaurant Game. One child plays the waiter and must remember the orders to be given to the cook.

25. Have the child learn short nursery rhymes, poems, or songs and repeat them. Additional verses may gradually be added. *Oh What Nonsense!* by William Cole may serve as a source.

26. Have the child say the alphabet through. Then isolate three letters such as "vwx" and give these to the child leaving out the middle letter (v-x). Ask the child to supply the missing letter. Words, numbers, days of the week, and months can be substituted for the alphabet letters.

27. In a small group, have the first child start a story with one sentence. Have each child repeat the previous sentence and add another related sentence to the story. Continue. Complexity and length of a story is determined by the individual children within the group.

28. Have a child be the official class announcer for a period of time. He must listen to you tell him the announce-

ments which he then tells the class. Begin with simple announcements, move to more complex.

29. The teacher reads off a series of symbols, numbers, letters, words, etc. that contain two or more of the same symbols. The child is to select the duplications and name them: 7, 2, 9, 3, 7, 1; answer: 7, 7.

30. Children can be asked to repeat in sequential order numbers, letters, sounds, nonsense syllables, or unrelated as well as meaningfully grouped words. They can respond by an oral response to the teacher or on tape, through a written response such as circling the symbols which they have heard on a worksheet, or by writing what they have heard.

31. Say letters, words, or numbers in sequential order, asking the child to repeat them. Next, after starting a sequence, restate it, leaving out a unit. Ask, "What did I leave out?" Next, restate a sequence, adding a unit. Ask, "What did I add?" Finally, ask the child to repeat the sequence in reverse.

32. When dealing with numbers, the child can dial the numbers on a telephone. The child must repeat orally the pattern as he dials. (Single, double, or other multiple digits may be used.)

33. Read a story to the students. Then read several sentences and ask whether or not they remember hearing the sentence in the story they just read.

34. Read a complete sentence to the child. He repeats it. Then read it several times, omitting a different word each time. Have the child complete it, using the proper word for each reading.

35. Give a number or alphabet series out of order and then ask the child to repeat the series in order.

36. Have a child say his telephone number. Ask the next child in line to repeat the number.

37. Musical songs with many repeats in a sequential pattern provide interest. Tapping out the rhythm encourages listening for different patterns.

38. Have the children close their eyes for this exercise. Then perform the suggested tasks and have them tell what they

heard in the proper sequence. The teacher bounces a ball, knocks on the door, stamps on the floor. (This is also useful for auditory discrimination.)

39. Number Series Games. For example, "Listen to the series, repeat all but the first one." Or, "Listen to these numbers and say the one in the series that is the closest to ____ (a number)."

40. Ask the child to alphabetize a series of three or four words presented orally.

41. Repeating Activities: tapping out patterns, reciting patterns of numbers, speech sounds, syllables, words, phrases, and sentences.

42. Each child is assigned a word. The teacher reads a story. Every time the child's word is mentioned, he raises his hand.

43. The child has pictures in front of him. The teacher says four words. The children are instructed to choose the pictures which are the same as the words said. Then ask each child to arrange the pictures on his desk in the order in which they were told. (This is good for auditory and visual perception, also.)

44. Record tapes which the child may use individually. The content may be digits, words, or letters which gradually increase in complexity. A pause should follow each series, which allows the listener to repeat what he has heard, circle the appropriate answers on a worksheet, or write down what has been heard.

45. Learn songs which emphasize sequenced or ordered items. Example: "Ten Little Indians," "Band of Angels," "Old MacDonald," "The Farmer in the Dell," "This Old Man," "Mulberry Bush," "The Wheels on the Bus."

46. Have the child repeat the sequenced steps in an assignment that has just been given.

47. A small xylophone is placed before the child with large numbers or letters written under each bar. The child has a small mallet. The teacher presents number or letter series orally and the child must hit the correct bars in the correct sequence, the correct number of times, and in the appropriate rhythm. To begin, the teacher may want to

emphasize only one of the above at a time. (This is useful for auditory-visual association.)

48. The teacher presents orally to the child a series of items (numbers, letters, phonemes, objects). The child then arranges a number of cards that have the appropriate items clearly indicated on each card. (This is useful for auditory-visual association.)

49. The child writes a series of numbers or letters on the chalkboard. He is then asked to erase them and repeat the series vocally. The numbers or letters he writes on the board can be from his own imagination or dictated by the teacher or one of the students. Another dimension to this would be that after he writes the sequence, he turns from the chalkboard and arranges a group of cards with the appropriate symbols or pictures in the proper order. (This is useful for auditory-visual association.)

50. The child responds to auditory and visual directions of the teacher. Example: The teacher may slap his hands together hard two times and once softly while saying: "Hard! Hard! Soft!" The child responds by saying the words and slapping his hands simultaneously in the correct rhythm and sequence. The sequence can be extended. The visual component may be removed. It is hoped that the large muscle movement will help improve auditory memory.

51. Read aloud the names of different objects, including three or four different categories. Ask one child to remember the boys, another the foods, etc. (This is useful for auditory perception.)

52. A sentence is read to the child and he must repeat it verbatim. Then, the teacher reads the sentence leaving out a word (or more) and the child is to complete the sentence. The sentences are to increase in complexity and length as the child progresses.

53. The child observes a picture while the teacher is reading a story that relates to the picture. The child must remember the objects told about in the story, or note extraneous objects or characters in the picture but not in the story. (This also can be used for visual perception.)

54. Have the child reproduce a series of movements presented orally (run, run, hop).

55. Arrange a dozen small toys on a table. Have one child stand by the table to be the clerk. Choose one child to call the "store" on the telephone and say, "I want you to send me a red ball." The clerk brings the red ball to the customer. Later, the number of items ordered may be increased.

56. Tap out an irregular sequence of three to five taps and have the children imitate the series: tap-tap-rest-tap-tap.

57. "First Letter Only" is a brief auditory memory exercise in letter discrimination. The teacher explains to the students: "I am going to spell a word by giving you a sentence. The word I want you to spell is made from the first letter of each word in the sentence." The sentence given might be, for example, "William is too hot." The answer would be *with*. At first the sentence may be written on the chalkboard. Later, as the children become more familiar with the technique, the teacher may dictate it. (This is useful for auditory synthesis.)

58. Tell the students the following story:

"I live outside of town, and here's how to get to my house from the town square. Imagine the road that leads from the square to my house as the letter Y. The town square is at the bottom of the Y. As you leave the square and go along the street, you'll notice the red brick library on your right. Soon you'll see a hotel over on your left.

"Keep on going down the road until it forks to form the two arms of the Y. Just before it divides, you'll see a sign hanging over the street. It says, 'You are leaving Wilson City. Come back.'

"Right where the road splits is a gas station. The road that goes left here runs out to Mountain Drive, and the one that goes to the right leads to Valley Highway. Turn right. You'll see my house on your right just before the road reaches Valley Highway.

"While you're here, we might visit my uncle, who

lives on the fork of the Y that goes left when you leave town. His house is near Mountain Drive."

Check on Listening Skills: Now let the pupils look at the papers you've distributed. Say, "This Y-shaped diagram represents the road your friend spoke of. Look at the letters on the diagram. Find the one you think shows the location of the sign that hangs over the street. Write that letter after your number 1." Give the youngsters time to call up the images they have made, and to decide which diagram letter is correct. Then continue:

"After number 2, write the letter that shows where the hotel is."

3. "Write the letter that shows where your friend's uncle lives."
4. "Write the letter for the town square."
5. "Write the letter for the gas station."
6. "Write the letter for Valley Highway."
7. "Write the letter for the library."
8. "Write the letter for your friend's house."
9. "Write the letter for Mountain Drive."

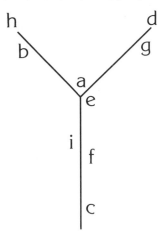

Have the children check their own papers. Answers should be: 1. E; 2. I; 3. B; 4. C; 5. A; 6. D; 7. F; 8. G; 9. H. You might read the directions again to let pupils check whether they visualized accurately. This exercise is adapted from *Language and How to Use It,* Book 2 (Scott Foresman).

59. Tape sentences. For example, "The girl ran away." Prepare a master with the same sentences that are on the tape. The child listens to the tape and uses the copies to read along silently. After each sentence on the tape is heard, ask a question, such as, "What did the girl do?" On the master, have pictures from which the child can choose an answer. He circles the picture that will answer the question. After he is able to respond correctly by circling pictures, words may be used on the master instead of pictures. Later, oral or written spontaneous responses may be given. The procedure may be lengthened to include paragraphs and short stories.

60. Present a picture, such as a bus. Give the child three verbal choices: "This is a taxi. It is a car. It is a bus." The child raises his hand when he hears the correct phrase. Increase the difficulty of the choices by adding a descriptive term, i.e., "this is a large bus; this is a bus that is filled with people." Verb tenses and adverbs may also be used.

61. Telephone Game. Whisper a short sentence to the child. He then whispers the idea to the next child in line. The repeating process continues until it reaches the last child who must say the idea aloud.

62. Give the children three chips of different colors. Call out the colors and have the child arrange the chips in that order. Shapes, objects, or pictures may also be used.

63. Give the child a series of numbers or letters. Ask the child to answer questions about them, either orally or in written form. Sample questions might be "What was the first number?" "What letter was last?" "What letter came before *s?*"

64. Use mnemonic devices, i.e., HOMES, the names of the five Great Lakes.

65. Use building sentences: "I saw a man" . . . "who went to the store" . . . "to buy some vegetables" . . . "that were very fresh." Each child adds on a phrase, but then must repeat the entire sentence before the new phrase can be added.

66. Use paper and pencil to perform the directions given orally: "Listen to these numbers and write down the fourth one." "6-2-4-1-7."

67. Have the students restore the correct order to sentences in which the order of words was presented incorrectly verbally. "The ran boy." The length of the sentences can be increased.

68. A built-in delay helps develop auditory memory skills. The student should not be allowed to respond to a direction until a specified temporal delay. "When I say go, draw a line under the fourth word on the line." (pause) "Go."

69. Have the child repeat directions that have been given before initiating action to follow them.

70. Taking notes on the material to be learned while trying to memorize the same information uses visual and kinesthetic feedback to assist in retention.

71. Make treasure maps for each child. Prepare instructions and read them one at a time, using a significant pause after each direction. Children follow the directions to find the treasure on their maps. The speed of presentation and complexity of the directions would be increased as the child shows improvement. The pauses would also shorten.

For the exercises given that require feedback of digit span, nonsense rhymes, words, etc., a tape recorder with headsets could be useful, so that the stimulus symbols could be previously recorded and used by the individual student determined by his own need.

CHAPTER 4

Auditory Perception

Introduction

Auditory perception is defined as the ability to receive and understand sounds and words. A child's hearing acuity as measured in audiometric testing may be within normal limits, but comprehension of auditorially presented sounds and words is weak. Auditory perception has a key role in the development of efficient reading skills, processing incoming verbal information, conceptual development, basic communication, social relationships, and in the ability to respond in an appropriate and safe manner to the environment. Auditory perception is basic to the verbal communication skills that are integral to the development of all interpersonal relationships.

Various aspects of language learning can be affected depending on the severity of the auditory perception problem. The child has difficulty in attaching meaning to words, understanding directions that are given, deriving full benefit from group discussions, acquiring abstract meanings, understanding words showing relationships, or fully comprehending questions asked. Receptive vocabulary is poor. He frequently asks for repetition when oral instructions are given. His response to auditory stimuli may be completely unrelated to the original questions or discussion. He probably prefers television to the radio or listening to stories read aloud. He may be able to repeat what he hears, but understands little of what he said. The child often uses gestures instead of words to convey the complete thought. He may misunderstand all aspects of multiple-meaning words. The meaning of words expressing a concept or an emotion are often difficult for this child. Problems can occur with quantitative terms, directional words, and prepositions.

Different areas and degrees of impairment may be affected by an auditory perception problem. Some children will be unable to understand the most concrete of words (doll, girl, bus). Others will acquire this concrete meaning, but have difficulty with abstraction. Adjectives showing relationships may be difficult. Problems may occur with quantitative terms (big, little), numbers, directional words (far, near, left, right), or place designations (on top of, under). Inaccurate perception of auditory stimuli can yield inappropriate motor responses and faulty social relationships.

If a child shows a deficit in auditory perception, one-concept phrases and sentences should be used. Ask only short questions; use experience charts in reading; and give visual cues whenever possible.

A child can be helped to attach meaning to auditory symbols of increasing difficulty by such means as: presenting the same words over and over until internalized, but using the words in a variety of contexts rather than straight drill; programming material so that new items build on previously learned material; limiting the vocabulary that is meaningless to the child; and by making the vocabulary meaningful by planned repetition of those words that are essential for the child to learn. Initially, visual cues often need to support the auditory stimuli to make meaningful interpretation possible. The teacher must consider the length of the verbal stimuli, the conceptual level of the words used, and the complexity of the sentence structure when planning remediation for the auditory perception area. Caution must be exercised when determining if an auditory perception problem actually exists when assessing a student's responses to the auditory stimuli presented. A meaningful response is possible only when the verbal information is within the student's experience base.

Tests that may be used to assess the auditory perception process are:

Cooperative Primary Tests
Test for Auditory Comprehension of Language
Test of Auditory-Perceptual Skills

Tests of Language Development-2

Test of Early Language Development

Detroit Tests of Learning Aptitude (oral commissions and oral directions subtests)

DTLA-3

Durrell Analysis of Reading Difficulty (listening comprehension subtest)

Receptive One-Word Picture Vocabulary Test

Durrell-Sullivan Reading Capacity and Achievement Test

Screening Test for Identifying Children with Specific Language Disability

Gates-MacGinitie Reading Test

Test of Auditory Analysis Skills (TASS)

Readiness Skills Tests (listening comprehension subtest)

Northwestern Syntax Screening Test

Katz Auditory Screening Test

Screening Test for Auditory Perception (STAP)

Brown Carlsen Listening Comprehension Test

Flowers-Costello Test of Central Auditory Abilities

Kindergarten Evaluation of Learning Potential

Illinois Test of Psycholinguistic Abilities (auditory perception subtest)

Murphy-Durrell Reading Readiness Analysis

Peabody Picture Vocabulary Test (PPVT)

American School Reading Readiness Test

Carrow Auditory-Visual Abilities Test

Assessment of Children's Language Comprehension, Revised

Kaufman ABC Battery (mental processing subtests)

Pre-Kindergarten Test of Central Auditory Abilities

Pupil Record of Educational Behavior (PREB)

Token Test for Children, Revised

Language Processing Test

MUMA Assessment Program

Binet and *Wechsler* test items, such as identification of objects by use and name, parts of the body, or the comprehension and similarities subtests (Although some of these items are contaminated by visual reception and verbal expression, they can still be used in the assessment process.)

Remedial Exercises

1. Play a tape recording containing various environmental sounds. Have the child close his eyes and identify what is happening. (*Sounds I Can Hear,* Scott Foresman & Co.) (This is good for auditory discrimination, also.)

2. Rhythm band instruments are best identified auditorially before they are presented visually. Have the children close their eyes and describe the sound they hear. A variety of instruments should be utilized.

3. The child is asked to make a sound using different parts of his body. The teacher may ask the child to make a sound using his hands, clapping; using his feet, stamping; using his fingers, snapping. The child may then be asked to make different sounds with these same body parts. A more difficult task would be "make a sound with your left foot and right hand." A puppet can be used to stimulate the game.

4. Blindfold a child and have him sit in the center of the room. Ask him to point to the direction from which the teacher is speaking. Move around the room silently and call him by name from several directions. This task may be varied with a drum or wooden block. Locations: front, front right, front left, right side, left side, above left front, above right front. Corresponding rear positions may also be used.

5. The child is to put his head on the desk. The teacher uses a noise-maker and makes some sounds to the right, left, behind, and in front of the child. The child is to point to the direction of the sound.

6. Make or tape record various sounds and ask the child to tell what is happening, such as tapping on various surfaces, dropping different articles made from a variety of materials. (This is useful for auditory discrimination, also.)

7. Coding. "I am going to give some directions. The children in these two rows will be 1-6-3. The children in the middle rows will be 1-4-1. Listen for your code number and follow the directions only if you hear them." (This is good for auditory memory, also.)

1-6-3	clap your hands	1-6-3	hop on your right foot
1-4-1	jump twice	1-4-1	raise your left hand
1-4-1	touch your knees	1-6-3	put your left hand
1-6-3	pull your right ear		on your right knee
1-4-1	stand up straight	1-4-1	stand on tiptoe
1-6-3	touch your left ear		

8. Present a story partially garbled by static or by having noise, garbled voices, music, or tappings, etc. in the background. Tell the child to listen to the story. Explain that he will be asked questions about the story when it is over. (This is good for figure-ground, also.)

9. Arrange mixed letters, numbers, or words on a tray. The teacher says "a," "e," "cat," etc.; and the student points out the proper symbol. This could be done by having the student circle the answer on worksheets or write what the teacher says on paper. In using worksheets, the teacher could give short directions, i.e., "Put a yellow box around 'team.' " This could carry the exercise a step further. For visual-auditory association, have student give the sound or word when he sees the card. For the more advanced, have the student use the sound in a word or the word in a sentence.

10. Use listening games, such as "Simon Says," and records such as "Let's Listen."

11. The group may like to play the game, Airplanes Fly (although the name can be changed to pertain to another concept). Direct the children to stand by their seats with their arms at their sides. When the teacher says, "airplanes fly," the arms should be raised and flapped as if the children were flying. If the teacher says, "tables fly," the children's arms must remain at their sides even though she may raise her own to try to catch them. Continue the game, directing the children to flap their arms only when an item is mentioned that can fly.

12. Children should be given directions for drawing activities. For example: a suggestion may be to draw a house. "Draw in three windows. Draw a chimney on your house. Color it green. Make smoke coming from your chimney." Or, directions might be in the form of actually constructing a drawing of something, such as a man, without the child

knowing beforehand what his drawing will eventually become.

13. Tape record various instructions on a tape recorder. The recordings would involve manipulative materials found in a small box. For example, "Find envelope 1, take the circle out, and put it on the flannel board. Find envelope 2, and put the white square on the circle."

14. Preposition Game. Ask the children to follow instructions: "Put the book under the desk." (This can be done with pictorial representations of the objects, or by using the actual objects.)

15. Read a story. Ask the child to raise his hand when he hears something silly. Later, ask the child what word was silly, and then what word should be substituted for the silly word in the sentences the teacher presented verbally.

16. Ask the child to answer "yes," "no," or "maybe" to questions: "Can you pick up a house?" "Is a brick heavy?" "Do girls grow beards?" This increases a receptive vocabulary.

17. To continue building a receptive vocabulary, this exercise may be used. The child is asked to recognize subtle differences in words when the teacher gives a sentence verbally that contains an inappropriate word. The student picks out the inappropriate word or words, and substitutes the correct word for the incorrect. For example, "Mr Jones *dove* his *par* into the garage." (This is good for auditory discrimination, also.)

18. Book exercises. "Find page 29." "Show me the fourth paragraph on page 24." "Point to the last word in the second paragraph."

19. Ask the child to mark on a worksheet: "The first square in the second row; put an X on the tree; put a square around the third circle," etc. A variation of this exercise might be to prepare a worksheet showing objects with lines under them, X's on them, etc. The children are asked to point to the picture that shows: an X on an apple, a line under a tree, a circle around the yellow square, etc. Directions for these worksheets should increase in length, complexity, and in the concepts involved. Knowledge of functions, prepositions, and colors are expected in order to complete the exercises

successfully. Worksheets could use groups of different objects or a single object.

20. The teacher gives the verbal directions for folding a piece of paper into a particular design or decorating cookies in a particular way.

21. Opposite Game. The children are asked to do the opposite of what the teacher asks, i.e., "Hop on the right foot," (the child hops on the left foot).

22. Dictate words, phrases, or sentences. The child is asked to select a picture to go with the auditory stimuli. (This is good for auditory-visual association.)

23. Use a series of pictures. As the teacher describes an object (for example, a picture), or tells a story about the picture, the child holds up the appropriate picture(s). (This is useful in auditory-visual association.)

24. Tell a story. As the story is being told, insert the name of a child and ask him to do something, i.e., "It was a very nice . . . (Carol, touch your foot)."

25. Select or create a story where familiar animals are found repeated throughout. Assign each child the name of an animal and when the animal's name is mentioned, the child is told to give the animal's sound. (This is good for auditory memory.)

26. Read aloud a poem containing much auditory imagery. Discuss with the children the images that have been evoked. Simple poems should be utilized initially.

27. Ask the child to close his eyes and listen to the tone of the teacher's voice. The teacher should repeat one phrase or sentence, varying it in tone and temperment. The child should be asked whether the voice sounded angry, happy, surprised, or unhappy. This may also be done with pictures, with the child making his voice correspond to the way the picture looks.

28. Instruct the child to put a marble into a jar when he hears the name of an animal that lives in a particular place: house, farm, jungle.

29. Read orally a variety of sentences. After each sentence, have the child tell how it was read: softly, rapidly, loudly, slowly, happily, sadly, etc.

30. One child is chosen to be "It." He thinks of an object in the room without letting anyone else know what he chose. He describes it. The class has to guess what it is. This may be done through the use of pictures, rather than objects.

31. Present the child with a series of unambiguous pictures which appear on a single piece of paper. Say the appropriate word or words describing one of the pictures, and have the child point to the correct picture. (This is good for visual association.)

32. Here is a way to introduce understanding of a concept when extraneous elements are presented: Pass out four cards to each child: one large black square, one large white square, one small black square, one small white square. Tell him: "Pick up a square that is white, not black, and that is big," or, "Pick up the square that is big, that is black, that is on the right." Letters or numbers can also be used rather than geometric shapes.

33. Give a child an oral description of something. After the description, have him select the object or picture described. (The visual process is also involved.)

34. Using colored paper, cut out different colored squares. Paste on tagboard to make a parking lot. Draw spotlights at the bottom of the paper. Use colored toy cars. The child is given oral directions to move a particular colored car to a colored space on the parking lot or to drive the car to a green, red, or yellow light. This may be expanded upon to make a street map where directions are given for streets and turns. (The visual avenue is also involved.)

35. The teacher has a puppet. The teacher says, "My man is always different than yours." "My man is sad, but yours is _____."

36. Read each phrase and show the word that tells what kind of phrase it is: Who? When? Where? What?
    (1) one evening
    (2) at the store
    (3) at Christmas
    (4) Mr. Brown said

37. To help the child identify absurdities in sentences, ask him such questions as: "Would you wear mittens in

summer?" or, "Do dogs use forks to eat their meat?" The student may later be asked to substitute the word that does not fit with a better word of his choosing.

38. Read the book *The Hungry Thing* (Follett) to the class and show them the pictures. The hungry creature in this book asks for such things as *schmancakes* (not pancakes) and *tickles* (not pickles). The class tries to figure out what he wants to eat.

39. Read a story aloud to the child. Stop at regular intervals and have the child provide a logical continuation based on the full comprehension of details of the story thus far presented. When the child has sufficiently demonstrated this comprehension, the teacher may go on with the story by using the child's ideas to present the next section.

40. Have the children listen to the sound track of a film, and have him explain what happened. After this, the film can be shown again with the visual portion.

41. Teacher reads aloud poems or parts of a funny story, such as the Dr. Seuss series. Who?, Where?, When?, Why?, and How? questions are asked of the children.

42. Send one child out of the room. Place a small toy car or a tiny doll in full view, but in an unexpected place. When the child returns, tell him you and the other children will help him find the toy. Everyone is to clap louder and louder when he approaches the object, softer and softer as he moves away.

43. Have the children compare sounds made by ringing a cowbell and a jingle bell; blowing on a big horn and a little one; dropping an eraser and a block of wood; tapping on a desk and on a folded piece of cloth; by walking and then tiptoeing across the room; by slamming a door and closing it gently. Compare the ticking of an alarm clock with the ticking of a wristwatch.

44. After a story hour or poetry time, have the children note the stress on certain words: "I think *I* can." Which part did he say loudest? What part did the little boy say the loudest when he said, "And I can run away from *you,* I can, I can." This training should not interfere with the fun of the story. It should be just a casual remark or question before the children turn to their next activity.

45. Have the children listen to pitch of sounds by striking a note on the piano and then striking a note an octave lower. While the first note is being struck, ask the children to stand tall with arms above their heads; while the low note is being struck, ask them to stoop low.

46. Have the children listen to "The Three Bears," "The Three Billy Goats Gruff," and "The Three Little Pigs" to bring out differences in the pitch of voices. Have one child hide behind the teacher's desk while the other children call: "Who's been eating my porridge?" "Who's tripping over my bridge?" or, "Who's blowing down my house?" The hidden child then replies in one of the three voices and the listening children guess which bear, pig, or goat he is pretending to be.

47. One child stands behind a screen and shakes a rattle, turns an eggbeater, or sweeps the floor with a broom. The other children guess from the sound what he is doing. Work toward getting many responses. Ask the children what else the noise sounds like. (This is useful for auditory discrimination.)

48. Play musical records that suggest the sounds of nature. Have the children raise their hands when they hear a part that sounds like a waterfall, the wind, a storm, a bumblebee, thunder, and so forth. (This is useful in auditory discrimination.)

49. Develop interpretation of voice tones. Ask the children, "How would you say 'Oh' if you received a beautiful new tricycle? How would you say 'Oh' if you fell and hurt your knee? How would you say 'Oh' if you saw something scary on television?" Later, have a child dramatize "Oh," and the rest of the children guess what feeling he is trying to show.

50. Arrange the children around the chalkboard. Have them close their eyes and try to guess the object drawn on the board. Use simple shapes at first. As the children are able to complete this activity, they may be tried on familiar words. (This is good for auditory discrimination.)

51. Traditional Show and Tell experiences can be used if the child is asked to *describe* in detail: color, function, etc.

52. The teacher can place a random assortment of objects before the child and ask the child to sort them into a specified number of groups. Color, shape, or function may be used as criteria for sorting. The child should verbalize why objects are *alike*. (This is useful for visual perception.)

53. Present a collective picture. Describe something in the picture. The child is asked to find that object. (This involves visual perception, also.)

54. Tape some sentences. On a worksheet have corresponding sentences that differ in some way. The child has to tell if the auditory and visual sentences are the same or different. (The tape may be replayed except if you are testing for auditory memory, as well.) (This is useful in visual discrimination.)

55. Read a story to the student. Then read several sentences and ask whether or not the sentence belongs to the story just read. (This is useful for auditory memory, as well.)

56. Have the child clap or raise his hand when he hears a word that belongs to a particular category. "Clap your hands when you hear the name of a vegetable."

57. Read a list of sentences to the child. Tell him to listen for a sentence that answers the question "Where?" Tell him to raise his hand when that sentence is read. "How-, who-, what-, and when-" sentences should also be employed.

58. Have the children depict the meanings of the sounds they heard during the day in picture format. This may be done after a short time of listening; or it may be used as a memory exercise as well by having the drawing performed at the end of the day, thereby summarizing the total day's sounds rather than the sounds of a given short period.

59. Read a description of a scene to the class. Encourage the youngsters to draw pictures from what they heard.

60. After hearing a song, ask the children to describe orally the story behind the song's words.

61. Rephrase questions to ensure more appropriate responses: "Did you help your father yesterday?" is better than "What did you do yesterday?"

62. State a sentence with faulty meaning and ask the child to correct it. "In the fall, we rake the snow."

63. Speak slowly, but not overly exaggerated. It seems that the sound unit representing the name of an object is so short that some children are unable to grasp it during normal language flow.

64. A communication game for older students may include teams of students. The "sending" team has a configuration using basic shapes. The "receiving" team tries to draw the same configuration using instructions given verbally by the "sending" team. The game can be modified to use cues and feedback between the two teams.

Example:

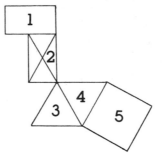

CHAPTER 5

Auditory-Vocal Association

Introduction

Auditory-vocal association involves the ability to draw relationships from what is heard, and then to respond verbally in a meaningful way to these spoken words. The child must be able to understand the auditory stimuli before vocal expression can be used effectively. Vocal expression is a part of most school activity, but the development and expression of ideas is often lacking. The type of auditory-vocal association problem described here is not a result of differences in speech patterns that create atypical syntax and give different meanings to words due to cultural or linguistic styles.

The child with an auditory-vocal association disability has difficulty in completing simple sentences or responding to riddles. He also has difficulty in remembering words for use in spontaneous speech. He often does not respond accurately to a verbal question. When he does respond, he may take a long time. He needs time to "think" about the auditory stimuli presented. A child who has this disability may also have a difficult time in classifying isolates into groups, in making generalizations, and in detecting absurdities. Weak abstract reasoning and concept formation may also be in evidence. A defect in auditory-vocal association is also based on the child's inability to draw relationships from what is heard, to manipulate the symbols internally, and then, to respond verbally. He may have difficulty holding two or more concepts in mind and considering them in relation to each other.

The child's conceptual base can be expanded through auditory enrichment in giving broader meaning to words by: using the words in varying contexts; verbally reactivating experiences the child has had; talking about and relating past experiences to present ones; using synonyms to expand verbal concepts; defining objects by telling what they are not as well as what they are; and by helping the child understand that the generalized concepts of words, such as "tree" refers to palm, evergreen, fruit, large, small, etc.

In the initial steps of remediation, it is important that the auditory stimulus be carefully timed with the experience. Children should be taught to listen and respond verbally in meaningful ways through the use of association, logical inference, and judgment. Expressive fluency should be recognized as a secondary goal.

If a child shows a deficit in this area, these remedial suggestions may be used:

1. Ask one-concept questions.
2. Provide visual cues wherever possible to reinforce the spoken word (e.g., filmstrips, slides, pictures, chalkboard work, three-dimensional materials).
3. Give ample time for responses.
4. Give the child a written question to think about before calling upon him to answer it orally.
5. Use short sentences and simple directions.
6. Permit short answers from the student.
7. Teach through concrete objects before attempting abstractions.
8. Develop the pupil's responsiveness by having him imitate simple actions or imitate actions in a story that has been orally read to him.
9. Play the game "Charades."
10. Ask questions using multiple choice answers within the stem. ("Do we draw a picture with a pencil or scissors?")

The auditory-vocal association area can be assessed through the use of the following tests:

Test for Auditory Comprehension of Language
Tests of Language Development-2

Test of Early Language Development
Test of Adolescent Language-2
Illinois Test of Psycholinguistic Abilities (ITPA) (auditory vocal association subtest)
Detroit Test of Learning Aptitude (free association and verbal absurdities and likeness and differences subtests)
Cooperative Primary Tests
Wechsler Intelligence Scale for Children-Revised (WISC-R) (similarities subtest)
Clark Madison Test of Oral Language
Parsons Language Sample (intraverbal subtest)
Robbins Speech Sound Discrimination and Verbal Imagery Type Test

Remedial Exercises

1. Riddles: "I am an animal and I have a long trunk." (elephant) "I am an animal, my baby stays in my pocket, I hop when I walk." (kangaroo) This activity can be changed by giving each child his own picture animal to describe in his own riddle.

2. The child can wear a picture of an animal on his forehead. He begins to ask questions about animals to gain more information about the one he is wearing. Other children can help him find out who he is through answers to his questions.

3. The teacher may recite some sentences and ask the child which words would be appropriate for completion of the sentences. Try to obtain spontaneous responses first, then the choices may be given one at a time.

    (1) "I can sleep on a . . ." (banana, bed, bike)
    (2) "I can eat . . ." (fruit, fur, fingers)
    (3) "I walk on my . . ." (hands, head, feet)
    (4) "I ride in a . . . " (car, chair, shoe)

4. The teacher may ask a child to select a word which does not belong after she has said the four words aloud.

arm	hat	coat	shoe
cart	wagon	voice	car
spring	summer	woodpecker	winter

tap	bank	school	store
swish	bang	bug	tap

Later, the child can explain why the one word was not like all the rest.

5. The following questions may be asked. They require only a "yes" or "no" answer. A more complete explanation may be given later.

    (1) If you walk on dry leaves, will you hear a sound?

    (2) If you throw water on a fire, will you hear a hiss?

    (3) Can you hear rain on the window?

    (4) Do you think an old rocking chair might squeak?

    (5) If a mouse crawls across wet paint, will it leave tracks?

    (6) Tell me other things that make sounds.

6. Ask the child to predict the outcome of the short stories. For example, "Grandfather and David went out to catch a fish for supper. Soon they each had caught a big fish. What happened next?" (If the child does not respond, the following choices may be offered to him. "Did the fish go for a swim? Did Grandfather milk the cows? Did Grandfather and David row to shore?")

7. Describe an object or picture in terms of its characteristics, functions, and/or uses, and have the child choose which object or picture was described. A store catalog may be used in beginning stages for providing visual cues. A "Talk Box" can be located in the room also, where everyday objects are placed to be described. By using an object or picture, ask the child what the use of each item is.

8. Ask the child to listen to three words at a time and tell which two go together. At first, supplement the auditory presentation with visual cues.

9. Use classification games with the children, discussing each item as it is identified as to why it is being placed in each category, i.e., how it is alike and different from other objects in the group.

10. Use word associations. Have the child name all of the things he can think of when you say, "mother," "play," "home," etc. Keep a list of his responses so he can see his progress.

11. The children should be asked to complete simple familiar phrases, such as, "My name is _____ ." "To learn to read and write, we go to _____ ."

12. The children should be asked to complete simple sentences with words missing in various positions of the sentence.

13. Opposite or synonym games can be employed.

14. Read several sentences and have the child choose and repeat the one sentence which is most relevant to a previously presented auditory cue.

15. Ask oral questions which would anticipate needs in various situations or answer the question of what would happen next.
    (1) "If you were going to bake a cake, what would you need?"
    (2) "What would you do if your dog was lost?"
    (3) "You spilled a glass of water; what would you do next?"

16. Categorizing questions should be asked. For example, pick an event, and ask the child to name everything he would bring to a picnic. Ask the child to name all the words he can think of that begin or end with a particular sound. (This is useful for auditory discrimination, also.)

17. Read questions and ask the child to decide upon an answer from those the teacher gives. "Which of these has a tongue, but cannot talk?" (man, shoe, radio)

18. Use analogies:
    Robin is to bird, as a poodle is to _____ .
    A shoe is to a foot, as a ring is to a _____ .
    Use analogies using numbers (2 is to 8, as 3 is to _____); letters (h is to i, as r is to _____); materials (a tire is to rubber, as a window is to _____); whole-part relationships (a wheel is to truck as a sole is to _____); involving action (a dog is to running, as a rabbit is to _____); locations (a typewriter is to an office as a stove is to a _____).

19. Give the student a group of words and have him use those words in a meaningful sentence. The number of stimulus words may increase as the child improves.

20. Say a word and ask the child what it makes him think of

and what expression he associates with the word. This can be done by presenting visual cues, such as a picture, and asking the child what the picture tells us, what's happening, etc. (Pictures from the National Dairy Association are excellent for this activity.)

21. Read a short paragraph and ask the child to explain which sentence does not belong. (This is useful for auditory perception, also.)

22. The student can be given a stimulus word naming an object. He is then asked to describe the object, and then to create a story about it.

23. Inferential questions may be asked of the student concerning a paragraph or short story.

24. Two students can carry on a telephone conversation using props. Possible topics should be given to the students in the initial stages of the exercise. The class may listen and expand on points omitted.

25. Storytelling. A list of characters is written on the board. Select students to tell the story (a smaller number in the beginning). The first student sets the stage using the first character. As the story develops, each student adds to it by entering the next character on the list.

26. Let the child teach a lesson in geography. Select a particular place. Questions to be answered: What direction is it from where we live? How can you get there? What will the temperature be? How many miles away is it? What kind of animals will you find there? What are some of the customs of the people who live there?

27. Have the child pretend to be giving directions to a stranger on how to get to a particular place in town or describe how to build certain objects.

28. If the child can read sentences, ask a question like "Where do you live?" Then present the written sentence, "201 South Elm Street," for the child to read. Then repeat the question but do not show the sentence.

29. Use lotto games to develop opposites and synonyms. (Although lotto games emphasize visual perceptions, verbal responses can be built into the game and insisted upon.)

30. Using a hand puppet, the teacher creates various situations or events and the children must tell how the puppet felt. Example: "He found a dollar and bought the toy he had been wanting." (This is useful for auditory perception, also.)

31. The teacher makes a collection of items that are basically used in the same way or that are alike in size, etc. Ask the child to find two similar items. Then ask why they are alike. Alternatively, one child chooses a friend to stand beside him. He tells how they are alike; the other tells how they are different. The first child then sits down and the second chooses another child, and the exercise is repeated.

32. Each child is assigned a room in a house or section of a department store. As the teacher calls out the name of a piece of furniture or other object, the child whose room or department it best belongs in tells the teacher. As the child is selecting the best room or best department, he should be vocalizing "why" he is grouping it as he is.

33. The teacher tells a story describing a certain place. The children close their eyes and raise their hands when they think they know the name of the place she is talking about.

34. Have the children tell about an art project they have made, a clay figure, a drawing, or painting.

35. Ask some "What would happen if?" questions. Example, "What if everyone had three fingers instead of five?"

36. The teacher asks the children how many ways they can use an object or thing, such as "How many ways can you use a brick?"

37. Three words are presented to the child to be used in a story. The child must relate the three words into the fabric of the story.

38. Three inch by five inch index cards are kept in a "story box." On each is written an unfinished sentence suitable for the beginning of a story. Each child draws a card and uses the unfinished sentence as a story starter. The stories may be informational (based on science or social studies), or imaginative.

39. Three words are presented to the child and he is to name

a category that would fit all three. The number of given words may be increased.

40. Take a field trip to the zoo, restaurant, store, museum, etc. On return, play a game of Twenty Questions relating to the experiences of the field trip. (This may be used as an auditory memory exercise if the relating of a sequence of events is desired.)

41. Obtain family photographs or slides. Ask the pupils to describe the event shown visually. (This is useful for visual association.)

42. Using cartoons or other pictures in sequence, ask the child to describe what is happening. (This is useful for visual association.)

43. Encourage descriptive word activity. Say, "I have a car." Ask the students to think of adjectives describing the car. Other objects may be substituted for "car."

44. Ask the children to vocally list all the things they can think of that can carry other things; that have ears; that can be built from bricks; etc.

45. A child may teach a skill or concept to other members of a class or children in lower grade levels. For example, have him verbally describe how to cut out and color geometric forms.

46. The children can play a word game in which one child begins with the first word he thinks of; the next one gives a word that means the same; the next an opposite, etc.

47. The children are asked to imagine they are somewhere, such as in a plane, riding down a highway, etc. The teacher then gives them oral sentences which they are to complete verbally. "The roads look like _____."

48. Verbally, give a series of related words, and tell the student to add a word at the end to show how they are related. Example: cake, coke, hot dog, popcorn (food).

49. Make a list of questions to be read orally and have the children answer them orally. Some examples are: "How many ways can a castle look?" "How many ways can a dancer move?" "How many ways can a person speak?"

50. Precise Definitions. "Here are some words. Let's tell as much about the word as we can so that everyone will

understand what the word means. For example, *orange.* You could say, 'A citrus fruit, orange in color, sweet in taste, has segments and seeds, has a thick, bumpy skin, grown on trees, is rich in Vitamin C . . .' "

51. A word-man calls out "bird, beast, or fish" (other groupings can be used such as, "fruit, vegetable, or meat"), and then says one of them, such as "bird," pointing to another player. The child must then name a bird, before the word-man counts to ten. This player then calls out a category. If the one who is "it" cannot think of a suitable word, he is out. If he repeats a word another player said, he is out. (This is useful for auditory memory, also.)

52. Categories. The players decide on a category, such as animals, places, food. The first player names an animal, for instance. The next player uses the last letter of the word for the first letter of his word. For example, *bear, rabbit, turtle.* (This is good for auditory discrimination, also.) A name may only be used once. (This is good for auditory memory.) If a player cannot think of a word, he is out of the game.

53. Read a sentence to the child. Then ask the child to say the same idea in as many different ways as possible. (This is good for auditory perception, also.)

54. Read a short poem or story to the children. Ask them to relate it to the class in their own words. (This is useful for auditory memory.)

55. Spin a bottle which has objects, cards with words on them, or pictures inside. When the bottle stops, the child at which the opening is pointing selects an object, word, or picture, and names it. After this, a child responds using the word in a sentence, describing the object, etc.

56. Orally, give the child a name of an occupation, and ask him to tell what kind of work is done and what sorts of tools the person uses to accomplish his work.

57. Use a deck of cards with words written on them. On his turn, each child takes a card, says the word out loud, and uses the word in a sentence to start a story. The next child proceeds, adding to the story. (This is good for auditory memory, also.)

58. Present scrambled sentences to the child. He is asked to

unscramble them without the use of pencil and paper, and recite them in their appropriate order, orally. (This is useful for auditory memory and auditory perception, also.)

59. In categorizing, we should try to develop in the child the concept that the best way to convey meaning is through being specific.

> If I mention words . . . car, plane, train, bus (transportation)
>
> To be more specific I can say: sedan, station wagon, convertible (type of car)
>
> To be more specific: Chevrolet, Buick, Ford (make of car)
>
> To be even more specific: Stingray, Ferrari, 240-Z, Lotus (sports car)

60. Puzzles. Instruct each student to take apart a puzzle, putting the pieces into various groups. He must verbalize about each piece as he is removing it and why he is placing it with the other particular puzzle parts.

CHAPTER 6

Auditory Synthesis

Introduction

Auditory synthesis, auditory closure, or sound blending, involves the ability to combine smoothly all the sounds or syllables of words to make them a whole, or the ability to analyze a word into its separate sounds. This skill, as well as auditory sequencing, is closely related to the reading and spelling process. The child having difficulty in this area may misspell words, leaving out parts. He will often be unable to pronounce smoothly syllables of a word without breaks among them. The child may be quite familiar with the individual sound elements, but he cannot blend them to make a smooth pronunciation of the word. He may sound only the first symbol or two in a word and guess at the rest. He may sequence the sounds or syllables oddly. Recognition of the same sounds in different words will present a problem. This child often cannot break words into syllables or into individual sounds. Those with synthesis problems cannot combine parts of words to form a whole. This child will probably have difficulty in independent word attack skills. Blending isolated parts or words into meaningful wholes or blending sounds into words is an important skill in learning to read. If a child has difficulty, he may not understand what is expected of him. He may not perceive the parts as they relate to the whole; he may not be able to remember the parts; or he may not be able to combine the auditory units into the correct motor sequencing for speech. The student may be a slow, over-analytical reader who fixates on each and every letter.

Auditory synthesis depends on such factors as: the frequency and recency with which the child has heard the expression; the number of choices possible; the position in the expression of the parts omitted; and the number and length of the parts omitted.

Several procedures have been used to teach auditory synthesis. Each has certain advantages and disadvantages. One factor in the ease with which sounds can be blended into words is the rate at which they are presented. The closer they are presented in time, the more readily they will be blended. If the child cannot blend sounds at a one-half-second interval, ask him to repeat the word after you, then to repeat it when you say it very slowly. "What is this word?—tr-ee." If the child cannot respond "tree," ask him to say, "tree." Then, "What is this?—tr-tr-tr-ee-ee," with each sound prolonged but the two sounds running together. Then try another two sound word. When the child has learned to blend two sounds with a short interval between sounds, present the sounds at a slower and slower rate until he can synthesize them into a word when presented at two-second-intervals. According to Kirk, "the reason for teaching the child to blend sounds at a two-second-interval is that when he uses the phonetic system to read, a beginner requires two seconds to recognize a visual letter symbol; recall the sound associated with it; hold the one sound in his mind while he translates the next visual symbol into a source for sound."[1]

Another approach is letter-by-letter sounding. Letter-by-letter sounding teaches a left-to-right sequence. However, extraneous sounds may distort the sounding, particularly the addition of an *uh* sound to consonants, cuh-a-tuh. (cat).

Other approaches are: the sounding of the initial consonant while the rest of the word is sounded as a unit or spelling pattern of two or more letters, "c-at." Words with the same final phonogram are taught as word families. In this approach, the initial consonant and following vowel are sounded as a unit and the final consonant is added as, "ca-t." This latter method appears to avoid extraneous sounds, makes blending easier, and prepares the way for syllabication of longer words.

Other points of technique when discussing auditory synthesis to be remembered are:

---

[1] *Thorlief G. Hegge, Samuel Kirk and Winifred Kirk, Remedial Reading Drills* (Ann Arbor, Michigan: George Wahr Publishing, 1955).

74

1. Avoid extraneous sounds when blending.
2. Words should be sounded continuously, i.e., the sound of one letter running into another letter.
3. Pronounce the whole word, then pronounce it successively more slowly until the individual sounds are given separately. Then reverse the process, starting with separate sounds, speeding up gradually, so that the relation between the separate sounds and the usual pronunciation of the word is heard.
4. Keep the duration of lessons in auditory synthesis short, about ten to fifteen minutes.

Forms of sound blending exercises include compound words, two-syllable words, short words containing long vowels, short words containing short vowels, and short words that sound more alike, auditorially. After the children are successful with short words, longer words of each type may be presented.

The following tests may be used in diagnosing a child with an auditory synthesis problem:

Kindergarten Auditory Screening Test
Illinois Test of Psycholinguistic Abilities (ITPA) (sound blending subtest)
Gates-McKillop-Horowitz Reading Diagnostic Tests
Roswell-Chall Auditory Blending Test
Gates-MacGinitie Reading Tests
Readiness Skills (auditory blending subtest)
Katz Auditory Screening Test
Flowers Phonics and Blending Test
Goldman, Fristoe, Woodcock Sound Symbol Tests
Test of the Awareness of Language Segments (TALS)
Auditory Blending Test

Remedial Exercises

1. Have the child count the number of syllables in a word while you say it slowly. The child can also tap the syllables and accent as he hears them. Tokens or chips can be used to show how many sounds are heard. Vocabulary familiar to the child should be used.

2. Have the child listen to the word while you say it in parts such as, "pa-per," "cray-on," "bas-ket-ball," etc. Then have the child point to the objects in the room and say the name as it is usually pronounced. He may also point to pictures.

3. Say a list of words to the child by syllables. Have him repeat the words without breaking for syllables. Begin with compound words: "base-ball"; expand to two sylla-ble words: "af-ter"; short words with long vowels "t-a-k-e"; short words with short vowels: "p-a-n"; and short words with similar sounds and configurations: "cap," "cat," "can."

4. Have the child count the number of sounds in a given word by saying it very slowly and making a mark on the paper or chalkboard for each sound. Then repeat the word to him slowly, sound by sound, and have him blend them together. After several practice drills, increase the rate at which the sounds are produced.

5. Show the child pictures of several objects. Say the name of one of the objects, sound by sound, so that the child has to blend them in order to find the correct picture. Clues for sound blending can be given without the use of pictures, also. The teacher can inform the child that the word about to be sounded is within a certain category. This narrows the choice of possibilities without the visual cues that require a recognition response. As the child progresses, visual and other auditory cues are eliminated. The child should be expected to identify the word the teacher sound blends without help, strictly through audi-tory synthesis.

6. Use kinesthetic letters (sandpaper, velour, pipecleaner), and have the child trace the letters as he sounds them. Cursive script which is connected would be more appropriate than manuscript for the blending principle.

7. Choose multisyllable words from the child's sight word vocabulary and write them on flash cards. Give him a card with only the first syllable from three or four cards. Have him say the word aloud as he tries to find it.

8. As a means of overlearning a short vowel sound, a sheet with a column of short *a* or *o* words are listed with an

explanatory picture at its right. Each word is missing a letter, the short vowel sound or the last consonant. These must be sound blended in order to recognize the picture and supply the missing letter. At first, this exercise should be used with only one vowel sound. Later, two or more review sounds may be mixed with the new sound. (This is useful for auditory discrimination, also.)

9. This is a sound blending exercise that can be modified to encompass various channels and processes. The consonant sounds the child is able to identify are placed in two columns and the vowel or vowels to be used or taught are placed between the two columns.

b		f
c	a	g
d		t

(1) The teacher is to point to a combination of letters, like *b-a-g*; and the child is to give the sound of each and blend them into a word.

(2) The teacher can say the sounds while the child is observing. The child must then point, say, or point and repeat them correctly and sound blend them into a word.

(3) If the child is slow at recall or retrieval of letter names or sounds, the teacher can speed up the process by pointing as quickly as possible, with the child immediately supplying the proper letter-name sound.

(4) This exercise can be used as a pure visual memory span drill by having the teacher point out a sequence of letters and have the child either repeat the sequence verbally or by pointing.

(5) This exercise can be used to identify whether an auditory-vocal problem is primarily auditory or vocal by changing channels in presentation and response types. For example, remove the visual cues and give the sequence orally and receive a vocal reply. Then give a series of letters orally and have the child point to the sequence (no vocal). Next, point out the sequence and the child is to give a vocal response.

Note the drill he has most difficulty with and determine if the problem is really just auditory, vocal, or a general problem.

10. Have the students respond to these questions:
    (1) "If b-a-r-n is *barn*, what is b-o-r-n?"
    (2) "If b-o-r-n is *born*, what is t-o-r-n?"
    (3) "If f-i-r is *fir*, what is f-i-r-s-t?"
    (4) "If b-u-r-n is *burn*, what is t-u-r-n?"
    (5) "If b-e-t-t-e-r is *better*, what is b-u-t-t-e-r, l-e-t-t-e-r, b-a-t-t-e-r?"
    (6) "If d-a-r-k is *dark*, what is p-a-r-k, s-p-a-r-k, m-a-r-k?"
    (7) "If y-a-r-d is *yard*, what is l-a-r-d, h-a-r-d, c-a-r-d?"

    Direct the pupils in the changing of various parts of words to form other words. Use leads such as those suggested above. Spell both the key word and the new word to be recognized by a pupil from the key word. (This is useful for auditory discrimination, also.)

11. The teacher begins by repeating a riddle such as one of these indicated below. The pupils listen to each riddle, give the answer word, and spell the word. If the pupils are capable, they may compose similar riddles on their own. (This is useful for auditory discrimination, also.)

    (1) I am thinking of the name of an animal.
        It is a short-*i* word.
        It begins with *p*.
        It ends with *g*.
        What is the word? (pig)

    (2) I know a short-*u* word that is the name of something to eat.
        You like it.
        It begins with *b*.
        It ends with *n*.
        Name the word and spell it. (bun)

    (3) I am thinking of a short-*i* word.
        It is the name of a boy.
        It begins with *J*.
        It ends with *m*.
        Name the word and spell it. (Jim)

(4) I am thinking of a short-*i* word.

　　It means the opposite of hers.
　　It begins with *b*.
　　It ends with *s*.
　　What is the word? (his)

(5) I know a short-*u* word that is the name of something to eat.

　　A squirrel likes it.
　　It begins with *n*.
　　It ends with *t*.
　　Name the word and spell it. (nut)

(6) I am thinking of a short-*a* word.

　　It is the name of a game.
　　It begins with the letter *t*.
　　It ends with the letter *g*.
　　Name the word and spell it. (tag)

12. A cutout of a train can be made having pockets or velour tape to hold various sounds. The engine would represent the beginning sound of a word, the car(s), the middle, and the caboose, the ending sound. As the child pronounces the separate sounds, he pushes them together to form a train.

13. Have the child place his finger under each letter as he sounds it and then sweep his finger under the whole word as he blends the sounds.

14. Plastic letters or cutout letters can be pushed together as the child is blending the sounds orally.

15. A strong sight word vocabulary should be developed.

16. Language Master cards may be used in the remedial exercises.

17. Display pictures of familiar objects. Then give the child the ending of a word: ＿＿ g. Let him choose the picture to complete the word *pig*. This exercise can be used where the beginning of the word is given, and the child chooses the picture to complete it.

18. Phonics exercises:

(1) Have the child circle the beginning, missing sound:

　　The old man was very ＿＿ oor. (b p d)

(2) Fill in the blank with a word that starts with the same sound.

(milk just food let)

| look | _____ | full | _____ |
| make | _____ | jump | _____ |

(3) Ask the child to fill in the same ending sounds.

(book take pump pull)

| look | _____ | jump | _____ |

(4) Ask the child to fill in the missing letter of a rhyme.

The boy went up the big, green hill.

When I'm sick I take a ___ill.

This ha___ makes me look fat.

(This is useful for auditory discrimination, also.)

19. The teacher presents the material to be used for sound blending in its entirety before asking the child to finish the incomplete form. "I am going to say the word bicycle. Now you finish it, 'bicy_____.'" Next, use the particular word in a sentence or phrase to give the correct context clue. "Peanut butter and jel_____." "Use a piece of chalk, and write on the black_____." Then, present familiar material in incomplete form. Ask the child to complete it without any clues. What word is this? "Croco_____."

20. Show the child a whole word. While he is looking at it, separate the letters, placing them about an inch apart. Take the first letter, say it, and at the same time move it toward the second letter; move them both toward the third, etc., while continuing to say the sounds while moving them together.

21. Prepare printed lists of words, and record the lists on tapes. The child looks at the words, listens to the tape, and then repeats them on the tape. Next, the teacher says each syllable, then the child says the same syllable on the tape where space has been left for this purpose. Then at the end, the child is asked by the tape to "say the whole word."

22. Read some sentences to the children in which they have to blend some speech sounds to make one of the words say, "We went to the s . . . t . . . or (e). Who can blend the

last word and repeat the sentence for us?" (This is useful for auditory memory, also.)

23. Adapt familiar lotto games. The teacher holds up a little card and slowly says the word pictured, "t-r-e-e." The child is asked to look on his big card to see if he needs the picture. If he does, he then is required to say its name and if correct, is given the little card.

24. Relate syllable learning to music. Have the children clap beats to syllables of words in familiar songs.

25. The teacher says, "I am going to ask you to do something. As soon as you know what it is, you may do it." For example, "You may 'c-l-a-p.' "

26. The teacher draws squares on the blackboard. In the left-hand corner of each is a consonant; and beside each, a list of phonograms. The children are asked to give the initial sounds and then form the words. (This is good for auditory discrimination, also.) For example:

h	at
	ay
	all
	ad

27. A word wheel can also be used showing blends and phonograms. The child would rotate the inner circle and read the words as they appear.

28. The teacher spells or phonetically sounds out the word, and the student must give the word. The teacher's oral spelling may vary considerably. He may give the sequence of separate phonetic sounds for each letter, and thus require the student to integrate the auditory sequence into the word. He may name the letters and group them in an unusual fashion, breaking apart normal phonetic blends. He may give the spelling by syllables, either in units of letters or merely giving the sound of the

syllables. He may simply spell the word, but with a full three- to five-second delay between each letter.

29. Prepare a tape in which one-syllable words are pronounced, i.e., "C-c-c-c—ome; l-l-l-l—ook; g-g-g-g—o"; and so on. The student is given a sheet of paper with words listed as follows:

1.	look	come	corn	cow
2.	stay	look	by	book
3.	toe	got	go	gone

As he listens to the tape, the student is instructed to circle the words he hears. At the conclusion of the tape, the student's paper should be checked immediately. If he misses any of the words, the tape should be played again and the procedure repeated. When this approach is first introduced, the teacher should select words to be listed on the sheet that are obviously different in appearance.

30. New Zoo is a gamelike approach to auditory synthesis which young children enjoy. The names of two familiar animals are blended to make a new word. For example, turtle and turkey could become a turkle, a lion and a goose could become a gion. The children can then draw pictures of the new "animal." The exercise offers an opportunity for the youngsters to use sounds in different ways and the pictures that follow are often delightfully funny.

31. Use larger "chunks" of words to blend.

32. Use movable one inch tiles with letters printed on them or Scrabble pieces. As the child begins to blend the sounds vocally, have him move the tile representing the sound being said next to the new sound needing to be blended.

33. Child can tap out syllables or beats in a word.

34. Have the child draw a word card from a group of cards all representing words containing blends. Ask the child to say the word selected and give another word which begins with the same blend.

CHAPTER 7

Auditory-Vocal Automaticity

Introduction

Auditory-vocal automaticity refers to the ability to predict future linguistic events from past experience. It implies correct and automatic grammatic and syntactic responses to our language system. A child with a deficit in this area has problems in responding to questions in a correct grammatic form. He has trouble with verb tenses, suffixes, and plural endings. He may also use small words incorrectly. This child presents relative slowness in language processing skills. His word order in sentences is frequently jumbled.

There is often a problem in identifying grammatical and syntactical errors in his own language or that of others. Environment can have an important influence here. The question to ask is, "What language models are available to him in the context of the home and family?"

If a child shows a deficit in the auditory-vocal automaticity process, these remedial guidelines may be followed for general classroom instruction:

1. Encourage imitation of correct grammatical expressions.
2. Visual cues should be provided to help initially in eliciting verbal responses.
3. Drill activities should be utilized to strengthen a sight vocabulary.
4. Exposure to good language models is essential.
5. Choral reading should be encouraged.

Remediation should also entail helping the child to automatically fill missing parts of what he partially hears. Listening to and repeating gramatically and syntactically correct language is one of the best and most consistent means for remediating the auditory-vocal automaticity problem. He must be helped to internalize certain redundancies from his experience. Extensive verbal practice should be given to those forms the teacher wants the child to internalize. Have the child use the desired forms through imitation, choral reading, dramatics, and spontaneous speech. The level of language used by the teacher in class would need to be gramatically and syntactically simple; phrases and sentences, short; and idioms, few in number.

Tests that can be used to assess auditory-vocal automaticity are:

> *Illinois Test of Psycholinguistic Abilities (ITPA)* (grammatic closure, audio-vocal association and auditory-vocal automaticity subtests)
> *Houston Test for Language Development*
> *Differential Language Facility Test*
> *Berko's Test of English Morphology*
> *Exploratory Test of Grammar*
> *Evaluation of Grammatical Capacity*
> *Carrow Elicited Language Inventory*
> *Test of Language Development*
> *Test of Early Language Development*
> *Test of Adolescent Language*
> *Parsons Language Sample*
> *Grammatical Comprehension Test*

Remedial Exercises

1. Tell the child to repeat and complete a sentence after the teacher. Visual cues may be used for additional assistance: "The color of the flower is _____ ."
2. Rhymes can be used, having the rhyming word obvious: "The fuzzy cat chased the _____ ."
3. Help the child develop the skill of "go-togethers": man and _____ (woman); peanut butter and _____ (jelly).
4. Language Master cards may be used. Draw or paste a picture at the left side of the card, then print a sentence,

leaving out the word. The child is asked to complete the sentence.

5. Use grammatic exercises such as the following:

2 day	a girl
2 days	a girls

   Yesterday, he talked to me. (use this for *ed, s,* or *ing*)
           talks

   Have the child supply the appropriate tense of a given word.

   Yesterday I _____ .
   Today I _____ .
   Tomorrow I _____ .

   The black airplane model is my favorite, but I have six ___ .

   I like to run, but _____ makes me tired.

   The dog found a bone

   All the dogs found _____ .

6. Read or tape a story and have the child fill in the suffixes *(ing, ment, able, ly)* after each appropriate word in the story.

7. Teach the child an incomplete sentence, such as, "This is a very nice _____ ." When the child has memorized this, walk about the room and point out objects saying, "This is a very nice _____ ." He should identify what you point out. Later, he should be able to recite the sentence, as well as supply the word.

8. Programed opening morning exercises requiring name identification, calendar activities, weather, etc., increase the auditory-vocal automaticity process.

9. Give the child a stimulus word and ask him to respond with as many different words as he can by changing endings. Cards with the endings written on them may be used for visual cues (*ed, ing, s, age, or, tain, tion, ful, less, ness*).

10. Use well known TV commercials. The teacher gives the first few words. The child then completes the commercial with the correct word.

    "Only you can prevent forest _____ ."
    "Try it, you'll _____ ."

11. The teacher gives a stimulus word to the child who is then asked to give a word that means approximately the same thing.

12. Present sentences where the root word can be changed by adding suffixes to complete the missing word, i.e., "Something that is used to freeze foods is called a _____ ." "Something that is used to grind meat is called a _____ ."

13. Various exercises on grammer usage can be used. (Many companies offer well made workbooks with practice drills in this area.)

14. To provide practice in reading and answering questions, record questions and appropriate answers on manila tag paper. Place them in mixed order in a card holder. Have the child select a question and read it aloud. The other child will reach for the answer in the "answer box." He reads it aloud, then he selects the response he feels is appropriate. (In the beginning stages of this exercise, the question and answers should use similar words.)

15. The teacher presents orally a short sentence in mixed order. The child then rearranges the words to make a correct sentence and presents it orally in its corrected form. This may be done in written form also by using blocks or cards with words written on them to develop appropriate sentences. Then have the child say the sentence and copy it. When the scrambled sentence is presented orally, auditory memory is involved.

16. Ask a question and have the children answer it by turning the question into a declarative statement. (This implies the changing of the verb form.)

17. Use Language Master cards with one idea sentences. The child repeats the sentence.

18. Show the child a picture of one object. "This is a shoe." Show him a picture of the same object, only more than one. "These are _____ ."

19. Have pictures in various frames on worksheets representing either the singular or plural form of the object pictured. The children then circle the picture word you say.

20. Verb forms, singular and plural words, comparative words, and prepositions may be drilled through the use of manipulative miniatures (dolls and doll furniture).

21. The teacher orally presents a sentence with an obvious structural or meaningful error, such as, "The book sat down and read the magazine." The children are to identify and correct the error. This can be done using inappropriate nouns, adjectives, or verbs. (This is useful for auditory perception, also.)

22. A story containing grammatical errors is read aloud by the teacher. The child calls out, "stop," each time he hears an error. The first student to do this explains what is wrong and earns a point. The teacher continues reading.

23. Present a picture of a cat eating. The teacher says, "The cat is eating his dinner." The child repeats. Then, present a picture of a cat by an empty bowl. The teacher says, "The cat ate his dinner." The child repeats. This could be easily turned into a Language Master exercise. (This is also useful for visual perception.)

24. Visual and manipulative helps may be given. Prepare cards with nouns, verbs, and adjectives familiar to the child. Group all nouns together on one ring, verbs on another, and adjectives on a third. Attach cards to a wooden or heavy cardboard stand. The child flips each card separately to form appropriate sentences. Sentence complexity may be increased by adding more card sets (articles, prepositions, conjunctions). Children should repeat the sentence orally for drill.

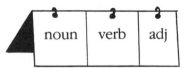

25. Engage the child in meaningful activity in the way of classroom jobs. Use controlled sentences to describe the action such as, "I am going to wash the blackboards," when the child is moving to do his job; "I am washing the blackboards," as the child is doing his job; "I washed the blackboards," when the child has finished his job.

26. Furnish a list of ten words to fill in the ten blanks left in a short simple story. Tell the child that he is to find the answers in the list of words and to fill in the missing words.

27. Read a sentence to the child, e.g., "The cat catches the rat." Then read variations of the sentence, leaving out a different word each time. For example, "The cat catches the _____ ." "The _____ catches the rat." "The cat _____ the rat," etc. (This is useful for auditory memory, also.)

28. Scrambled Sentences. Prepare a sheet of scrambled phrases. The child is asked to put them in order, 1, 2, 3, etc.

>   _____ made a cake.
>   _____ the little girl
>   _____ out of mud

29. Provide pictures showing past, present, and future actions. Ask the child to discuss the actions individually, and then to compare them.

30. Describe the activities of a child using "emphasized" tenses of the action words while the student is actually engaged in the activity.

31. Have the child complete sentences by filling in an omitted word or words in various positions in the sentences.

32. Unscramble parts of sentences so that they are in "correct" order.

CHAPTER 8

Auditory Figure-Ground

Introduction

The auditory world is made up of many sounds having many pitches, intensities, and meanings. The significance of these sounds is often determined by the individual as the sounds are structured to meet individual needs at particular times. An auditory process, figure-ground, relegates certain sounds into the background while selecting others as the focus of attention. An auditory figure-ground problem consists of difficulty perceiving relevant auditory stimuli in the presence of background stimuli or when there is a significant change in the intensity of the stimuli. For school success, it is not only important to screen out the distracting auditory stimuli, but the student must also learn to change the focus of attention at various times during the instructional day.

The student may have difficulty differentiating between relevant and irrelevant auditory stimuli. In many cases, there is reaction to the first recognizable element or focus upon isolated elements. An auditory/figure ground problem may be associated with inadequate discrimination due to the inability to adequately differentiate the essential from non-essential.

An auditory figure-ground problem has a direct relationship to listening. Listening requires the concentration of attention and anticipatory behavior about the forthcoming auditory activity. Good listening can only take place when the auditory stimuli are properly organized and structured. All sounds cannot be attended to with equal importance as all sounds, given a particular situation, are not equally important. Some are the focus—"figure"; and some are the background—"ground."

Students with auditory figure-ground problems cannot select the important speech sounds from the mixture of auditory stimuli and cannot structure the sounds selected so that they become ordered into units that are meaningful and distinctly different from all the other sounds. This problem causes a distortion in the total auditory experience.

In order to function in a standard classroom, the student must be able to perform three basic auditory figure-ground skills:

1. Distinguish school-related environmental sounds from general noise (a bell from noisy voices and clanging dishes in a cafeteria).
2. Select spoken language from environmental sounds (teacher directions from students walking around the class and the sounds from hallway passing time).
3. Attend to the important spoken words from a background of spoken language (teacher statement from a group of students talking).

An auditory figure-ground problem can also be described as a "competing message" problem. Some children with learning disabilities are adequate listeners under favorable classroom situations, but their attending and resultant comprehension decreases when there is competing stimuli. This problem adversely impacts on other components of auditory processing: auditory memory and auditory sequential memory. The child's problem becomes one of "selective attention," in that the ability to attend to relevant auditory information in the face of irrelevant auditory information is disrupted.

Interference from the background stimuli can adversely affect the student's attention, general behavior, social interaction, and the ability to learn. Without appropriate attending behavior to the necessary auditory stimuli, learning becomes confused and may even cease. The auditory figure-ground problem can have an even more adverse effect on the adolescent and young adult since it impacts more than educational performance. The problem can have a direct relationship to interacting socially, especially with non-learning disabled students in a standard program placement, and functioning appropriately in a community based work study placement. In vocational training, it is important that the student understand what is said when directions or specific instructions are given by the supervisor or co-employees.

Generally, remediation in this area can use several different approaches. One treatment program recommends a direct intervention approach to increase the student's tolerance for the background stimuli through the use of commercially available tapes or versions of these tapes developed by the learning disability teacher and/or the speech/language therapist. Through a compensatory approach, students are accommodated by the teacher's willingness and ability to control the environment, i.e., reducing the amount and/or intensity of the background noise in the learning environment and through specific procedures to gain the student's attention at particular times. Because of the nature of this particular auditory process, some students can engage in an internal figure-ground auditory sorting process only after their attention has been gained by visual or tactile cues. Another approach is the elimination or significant reduction of the background noise using right, left or bilateral ear occlusion using ear plugs or ear muffs. In summary, remediation directed toward classroom management aimed at enhancing listening opportunities will be beneficial to the student identified as having an auditory figure-ground problem.

If the student's suspected auditory figure-ground problem is present only under specific situations and not consistently, there may not be a true auditory figure-ground problem. The teacher should look closely at all factors that seem to be related to accomplishing the task when there appears to be a figure-ground interference. Such factors to consider are: the child's ability to understand the task (presented orally); clarity of the identification of the auditory figure stimulus; meaningfulness of the figure stimulus; meaningfulness of the compelling background stimuli; intensity of the background stimuli; intensity of the figure stimuli; the complexity of the stimuli involved; and past experience with the same figure/ground situation.

The auditory figure-ground area may be evaluated by the use of the following:

Auditory Selective Attention Test
Carrow Elicited Language Inventory
Goldman, Fristoe, Woodcock Auditory Skills Test Battery

Kindergarten Auditory Screening Test
Carrow Auditory-Visual Abilities Test
SCAN (auditory figure-ground and competing word subtests)

Continued performance testing (CPT) in the auditory mode using numbers, letters, or words depending on the age of the student may also be used. This procedure would require a child to attend and maintain the attention level on a task for extended periods of time using degrees of interfering background stimuli.

Remedial Exercises

Direct Approach

1. Play background music while the student is working independently for set periods of time (5-10 minutes). Increase the time as the student is able to respond appropriately with the music playing.
2. Help the child select relevant from irrelevant sounds by reducing potentially distracting visual stimuli by having the child cover his eyes.
3. Use tapes and records to begin to develop sound selectivity using cue questions before the audio is heard or identify questions after the audio is heard.
4. Condition the student by introducing sound into the structured learning environment on a selective basis varying its intensity and complexity and at the same time requiring attention to a particular auditory stimuli.
5. Ask the student to keep a log of the classroom disturbances. Discuss the situations named with the child to increase awareness of the background noise conditions that interfere with his learning.

Compensatory Approach

1. Give preferential seating to the student away from the background noise, i.e., a seat away from the major traffic pattern of the room, away from the exits, and from the ventilation system.

2. Move towards the child, making visual contact, when attention is necessary and there is background interference.
3. Touch the child to gain attention to focus on a particular direction, activity, etc., when background noise is present.
4. Call the child by name before asking a question.
5. Provide a study carrel.
6. Provide the child with ear plugs for use when independent seat work needs to be completed.
7. Provide ear occlusion using one or a pair of ear muffs.

CHAPTER 9

Reading Skills
For a Child with Problems
in the Auditory Processes

Introduction

Reading is a visual symbol superimposed on previously acquired auditory language. Before a child learns to read, language learning depends almost exclusively on the auditory channel. Therefore, the language base upon which reading skills are built are dependent on the child's ability to use auditory processes.

The three aspects of the auditory processes that are most significant for reading are discrimination of particular phonemes within words, auditory discrimination of words, and auditory synthesis. These abilities are especially important to the development of word attack skills.

Auditory processing problems may affect reading in the following ways:

— inability to hear the similarities in the initial or final sounds of words
— cannot perceive the similarities in words, e.g., "fat" and "pat"
— unable to hear the double consonant sounds in consonant blends
— lack of discrimination of short vowel sounds: "ten, tin, ton"
— cannot break words into syllables
— cannot break words into individual sounds

- inability to combine parts of words to form a whole
- cannot remember the sounds for the printed symbols or the names for the printed word
- inability to detect rhyming element of words
- difficulty in distinguishing similarities and differences in sounds
- lack of retention of sounds or syllables long enough to make matches or blends
- inability to relate the visual components of words to their auditory counterparts
- does not relate a part of a word to the whole word
- inability to synthesize or analyze unfamiliar words

Children with auditory deficits tend to learn better by using visual and/or kinesthetic means rather than by auditory or phonic methods. Using a linguistic approach may also be successful. This approach aims at providing accurate sound-symbol consistency with opportunities to develop listening skills as well as support through the application of the learning principles of regularity, simplicity, and frequency.

Techniques for teaching reading to children who have auditory problems involve: look-say method, sight words, flash cards, configurational clues, context clues, Gillingham's approach to teaching phonics, theme-based reading activities involving home, family, the community and special activities, experience charts, and intensive remedial training in all auditory areas. It is important to remember that the isolated drills in the various auditory areas must then be directly related to the reading process.

It must be noted that the treatment of a functional reading problem must address the total reading activities, not merely one component such as the auditory.

Remedial Exercises

1. Use the whole word approach when initially teaching reading.
2. Show that what we speak can be written.
3. Show that spaces represent divisions among words.

4. Say titles of stories. Ask the child how many words he hears. Ask him to point to the words on the pages of his book. Have him point to each word as it is said.

5. Select words for a sight vocabulary that are in his spoken vocabulary. Select words that look and sound different. Nouns should be taught first.

6. Match the printed symbol to the picture or object. Then the teacher should say the word. The child should repeat the word, and point to the picture representing the spoken word, and then point to the printed word. Saying the word aloud should be done while he is tracing it.

7. Label nouns around the room using the above technique.

8. Verbs may be taught in much the same manner. Tell the child to perform the action: hop, jump, etc. Then show him the word in printed form. Keep saying the word as the above exercises are carried out.

9. The Language Master or Language Lab can be used to develop the child's basic sight vocabulary. The Language Master enables the child to see and hear the word at the same time.

10. Adjectives and prepositions may be taught through the use of action pictures. Commands may be written on cards so the child reads and then performs the action himself or uses manipulative objects. Worksheets for following directions can be used.

11. The child can listen to you read the sentence or short phrase first, looking at each word as it is read. He can then respond in the same manner. To aid this, a cutout cardboard spacer can be used so that each word is only seen as it is read. Example:

12. Experience stories can be used. If a word is not within the present vocabulary, a picture can be drawn above the printed word. The stories can be collected at the end of the week, reproduced by the teacher (preferably on a

primary typewriter), and distributed to the children as "take-home newspapers." Rebus stories can also aid the child in their beginning stages of reading.

13. The children should be taught to use configurational and context clues.

14. Ask short questions in testing comprehension and give ample time for responses. Sheets with important questions to be answered should be given to the child before he begins his reading.

15. Give visual cues whenever possible.

16. Use pictures to show the vocabulary being learned.

17. Color code common elements of words.

18. Teach verbs through action activities.

19. Make the sounds to be learned as visual or tactile as possible. Example: blow on the child's hand to show the difference between "wh" and "w."

20. Teach the child to make longer words (talk, talking, talked, talker); make longer words into two or three shorter words; or find smaller words in the large words.

Remedial work in the association of auditory and visual perception must be done when teaching reading to the child with problems in the auditory area. Exercises in sound-to-letter association should be incorporated.

1. The teacher dictates a sound and then exposes a picture having that sound. The teacher dictates a sound, the pupil picks up the picture card to match. The teacher dictates the sound, then shows the symbol for the sound.

2. The teacher dictates sounds, shows symbols. The pupil repeats the symbol name and sound. The teacher dictates sound. The pupil picks up symbol, and says name and sound. The pupil hears the sound on tape or Language Master card. The pupil sees the item on card or worksheet and replies orally on tape.

3. The pupil can respond to a dictated sound and visual symbol by tracing over the symbol with finger (sandpaper, pipecleaner, plastic link, velour, yarn, or felt letters).

4. The teacher shows a symbol; makes the sound. The pupil repeats. The teacher shows a picture card. The pupil makes the beginning, ending, or middle sound as

requested, and places the symbol in the correct position. The pupil separates the picture cards and gives sound of the beginning, ending, or middle of the word as requested; then places the symbol in the appropriate position.

The above offer suggestions for improving reading—an auditory-visual association process. While using visual cues for enhancing reading skills, remediation must still be continued in the auditory deficit areas.

For each student, remediation begins with a specific technique individually designed to meet an identified need. Different stages of development in the reading process and consideration of the student's age result in the need for different remedial procedures. Remediation, however, must be done relative to the particular deficits identified that are hampering the reading process. The child will read no better than the specific deficit will allow. Meaningful repetition and the use of materials at a high interest level must be considered when planning the instructional process. As deficits improve, a broader based reading program can be more effective and specific remediation can be more easily transferred to the total reading/language arts program. A "total" approach that uses the same words to read, spell, and write will be most successful as this type of approach ties the written and visual system together and links memory, perception, and linguistics for a student who has difficulty seeing associations and understanding whole-part relationships.

Summary

Learning in the home, community, classroom, or workplace involves attending to sounds, sorting the auditory stimuli into meaningful units, ordering these units, retaining them, and responding to them in a meaningful manner. In a school setting, students are expected to: respond to teacher directions and peer requests; listen to the important information in direct instruction as well as in group discussions; sort out the important from the non-important; retain the important information over a varying period of time; and give the appropriate responses in a timely manner. The meaningfulness of the auditory material presented, the length of the message, and the output expected of the student all impact on the processing of the information. Therefore, it can be seen that the auditory processes are integral to learning . . . academic, social, behavioral, and vocational.

CHAPTER 10

Commercially Made Materials

In addition to the activities listed on the preceding pages which aid in the development of the auditory processes, there are many commercially made materials that are available to be used in this remediation process.

The material on the market, for the most part, does not claim reliability or validity. Specific application with materials cannot be relied upon to teach specific skills. The materials themselves are not as important as *how* the materials are used.

In using the commercially prepared instructional materials, the teacher or clinician is limited only by his or her own creativity. The materials available will only teach skills if the teacher uses them in the light of the specific deficit or diagnostic test profiles.

Sample exercises previously presented illustrate how auditory skills may be taught in the special education program or standard classroom. The commercial materials listed on the following pages may be used for instructional purposes as they are based on some of the underlying remediation principles discussed and can also be used to supplement the remedial exercises described in the preceding chapters.

Books

Better Speech and Reading
(Expression Company)

The Big Book of Language Through Sounds
(Pro-Ed)

The Child's Book of Speech Sounds
(Expression Company)

Come and Hear: A First Ear Training Book
(Follett)

Dr. Seuss Books such as *The Cat in the Hat, If I Ran the Circus, On Beyond Zebra*
(Lew's Books)

First Steps in Speech Training
(Expression Company)

The Junior Listen-Hear Books
(Follett)

Kindergarten Rhymes
(World Book-Childcraft)

The Listen-Hear Books
(Follett)

Listen, My Children, and You Shall Hear
(Academic Therapy)

Listening Aids through the Grades
(Teachers College Press)

Listening to Go
(Lingui Systems)

The Listening Walk
(Thomas Crowell)

Noise in the Night
(Rand McNally)

The Noisy Book Series
(Harper and Row)

Rhyming Riddles
(Pro-Ed)

Riddles, Riddles
(Western Publishing Company)

Sentences for Dictation
(Academic Therapy)

Sounds the Letters Make
  (Little, Brown and Company)
Talking Time
  (McGraw-Hill)
Too Much Noise
  (Scholastic, Inc.)
Wake Up, City
  (Norman Lathrop)
What Am I?
  (Western Publishing Company)

Filmstrips and Accompanying Records

Listen and There are Sounds Around You
  (Harcourt, Brace, Jovanovich)
Little Things that Count
  (Eye Gate House)
Noisy Nancy Norris
  (Harcourt, Brace, Jovanovich)
Sight and Sound Discovery Trips
  (Eye Gate House)
Sight and Sounds Series
  (McGraw-Hill)
Sounds We Use
  (Ginn)
Think, Listen, and Say
  (Eye Gate House)

Games

Auditory Discrimination Game
  (Pro-Ed)
Consonant Lotto
  (Dolch Instructional Materials)
Grammar Can Be Fun
  (Lippincott)

Group Sound Game
  (Dolch Instructional Materials)

Group Sounding Game
  (Dolch Instructional Materials)

HELP 1, 2, 3 & 4—Language Games
  (Lingui Systems)

Listening Skills for Pre-Readers, Vol. 1 & 2
  (Educational Activities)

Phono Rummy and Five Sets of Games
  (Milton Bradley)

Play It by Ear Auditory Training Games
  (John Tracy Clinic)

Riddle-a-Rhyme
  (World Book—Childcraft)

Sound/Picture Match-Ups
  (DLM)

Syllable Game
  (Dolch Instructional Materials)

Syntax: Focusing on Verbs
  (DLM)

Vowel Lotto
  (Dolch Instructional Materials)

Instructional Aids

All Purpose Photo Library: Set 2
  (DLM)

Association Cards
  (DLM)

Auditory Familiar Sounds
  (DLM)

Auditory Initial Consonant Cards
  (Steck Vaughn)

Basic Word, Phrase and Sentences Cards
  (Steck Vaughn)

Bendable Figures
  (Creative Playthings)
Buzzer Board and Buzzer Pattern Cards
  (DLM)
Hand Trap Set
  (Creative Playthings)
I Try
  (Noble Publishers)
IZIT Cards
  (Pro-Ed)
Language Making Action Cards
  (Pro-Ed)
Let's Listen Cards
  (Steck Vaughn)
Library of Vocabulary Photographs
  (Pro-Ed)
Listening for Speech Sounds
  (Harper and Row)
Magic Cards, Consonant Blends, Digraphs, Vowels
  (Ideal)
Miniature Toys by the Pound
  (Creative Playthings)
Motor Expressive Cards, I and II
  (DLM)
Phono Cards
  (Academic Therapy)
Phono Word Wheels
  (Steck Vaughn)
Photo Grammar
  (DLM)
Photo Language Cards
  (DLM)
Private Lines (battery operated telephones)
  (Creative Playthings)
Remedial Reading Drills
  (George Wahr Publisher)
Rhythm and Sound Instruments
  (Creative Playthings)

Rolling Reader Blocks
   (Scott Foresman)

Sequential Picture Cards, 1, 2, 3
   (DLM)

Sight Phrase Cards
   (Dolch Instructional Materials)

Singulars and Plurals, Sets 1 & 2
   (DLM)

Sound Cylinders
   (Creative Playthings)

Stationary Figures
   (Creative Playthings)

Step Bells
   (Creative Playthings)

Stimulation and Conversational Cards
   (Pro-Ed)

Syntax Flip Book-Revised
   (Pro-Ed)

Tok Back Sound Reflector
   (DLM)

Vee's Verbs, Sets 1 & 2
   (Pro-Ed)

Webster Word Wheels
   (McGraw-Hill)

Word Blends
   (Dolch Instructional Materials)

Word Making Cards
   (Pro-Ed)

Instructional Kits

ACHIEV
   (Lingui Systems)

Easy Does It for Young Listeners
   (Lingui Systems)

Ginn Language Kit
   (Ginn)

Grammar Big Box
  (DLM)
Language Big Box
  (DLM)
Oral Language
  (DLM)
Peabody Language Kits, 1-4
  (American Guidance Service)
Phonics Big Box
  (DLM)
Photo Resource Kit
  (Pro-Ed)
Sounds and Symbols Development Kit
  (American Guidance Service)
Speech to Print Phonics
  (Harcourt, Brace, Jovanovich)
Word Analysis Practice Kits
  (Harcourt, Brace, Jovanovich)

Programs

Apple Tree Language Program
  (Pro-Ed)
APT: Auditory Perception Training
  (DLM)
APT II: Auditory Perception Training
  (DLM)
Auditory Discrimination in Depth (ADD)
  (DLM)
Auditory Discrimination Training Program
  (Pro-Ed)
Auditory Memory for Language
  (Pro-Ed)
Auditory Rehabilitation
  (Pro-Ed)
Central Auditory Abilities Training Program
  (Perceptual Learning Systems)

The Child Speaks: A Speech Improvement Program for Kindergarten and First Grade
(Harper and Row)

Cove School Reading Program
(DLM)

Decoding for Reading
(MacMillan)

Developmental Language Stories
(DLM)

Developmental Syntax Program
(DLM)

Distar Language Program
(Science Research Associates)

Distar Remedial Program
(Science Research Associates)

Early Childhood Enrichment Series: Learning to Develop Language Skills
(Milton Bradley)

Goldman-Lynch Sounds and Symbols Development Kit
(American Guidance Service)

Grammar for Teens
(Lingui Systems)

HELPSS: Helm Elicited Language Program for Syntax Stimulation
(Pro-Ed)

Junior Listen-Hear Program
(Follett)

Lessons in Syntax
(Pro-Ed)

Let's Listen Auditory Training for Speech Development and Reading Readiness
(Ginn)

Listen-Hear Program
(Follett)

Listen, Speak, Read and Spell
(DLM)

Listening Skills Builder from the SRA Reading Laboratory
(Science Research Associates)

Murphy Phonic Practice Program
  (Durell)
MWM Program for the Remediation of Language Learning Disabilities
  (based on the Illinois Test of Psycholinguistic Abilities)
  (Follett)
Phonemic Synthesis: Blending Sounds into Words
  (DLM)
Plurals
  (Pro-Ed)
PLUSS—Putting Language to Use in Social Situations
  (Pro-Ed)
Positives, Comparatives, and Superlatives
  (Pro-Ed)
Programmed Spelling (with cassette tapes)
  (Academic Therapy)
Question the Direction
  (Lingui Systems)
Reading Incentive Program
  (Bowmar/Noble Publishers)
Ready, Set, Listen!
  (Lingui Systems)
Rebuilding Language
  (Pro-Ed)
Semel Auditory and Processing Program
  (Follett)
Semel Program for the Development of Auditory Perception
  (Follett)
S.O.S.—Sound, Order, Sense
  (Follett)
Sound Foundations Program
  (DLM)
SRA Learning to Think Series
  (Science Research Associates)
Steps Toward Basic Concepts Development
  (Pro-Ed)
Structural Reading Series
  (Random House)

TSA Syntax Program
  (Pro-Ed)
Visual Aural Discrimination Series
  (Academic Therapy)
WH-Programs
  (Pro-Ed)

Records

Records may be ordered from a variety of sources including local educational supply houses.

Auditory Discrimination Training Kit
Basic Concepts Through Dance
Basic Training in Auditory Perception, Volumes 1 and 2
Building Verbal Power
Call and Response Rhythmic Group Singing
Child's Introduction to Sounds
Classroom Rhythms
Dance a Story
Developing Fundamental Language Patterns
Dr. Seuss Presents
Ear Training for the Middle Grades
Ear Training for the Middle Grades, What is Listening?
Early Childhood Rhythms, Songs, Skills, Volumes 10 and 12
Expressive Sounds
First Talking Alphabet, Parts 1 and 2
Fun with Speech, Volumes 1 and 2
Good Morning Mrs. Miller (unfinished stories)
Hand Rhythms
Happy Time Listening
Learning to Listen
Learning to Read with Phonics (workbook)
Let's Listen
Let's Sing About the Alphabet
Listen and Do (records and worksheets)
Listening and Moving
Listening Skills for Pre-Readers, Volumes 4 and 5
Listening Time
Listening Time Stories, Albums 1 and 2

Listening with Mr. Bunny Big Ears
London Phonics Program
Musical Sound Books
Pathways to Phonics Skills
Programmed Enrichment Songs for Exceptional Children, Set A
Reading Readiness and Number Readiness
Rhythms to Reading (books)
Saying the Right Word
The Silly Listening Book and Record
Singing Sounds
Songs for Children with Special Needs, Volumes 1 and 2
Sound Skills for Upper Grades, Volumes 1, 2, and 3
Sound Way to Easy Reading (wall charts)
Sounds I Can Hear (storybook)
S.T.A.R.S. Training Program
Teaching Children Good Manners and Behavior (unfinished
  stories)
Teaching Children Safety (unfinished stories)
Teaching Children Values (unfinished stories)
The Time Machine Series
Who Said It?
Words and Movement About Myself and Musical Games

Tapes

Advanced Central Auditory Training Program
  (Perceptual Learning Systems)
Auditory Discrimination and Auditory Confusion Training Program
  (Perceptual Learning Systems)
Auditory Perception Training, Discrimination, Memory, Imagery, Motor, and Figure Ground
  (DLM)
Auditory Training, Familiar Sounds
  (DLM)
Auditory Training, Rhythm Band
  (DLM)
Blends and Digraphs Structured Reading Tapes (worksheets)
  (Ideal)

The Bugs, the Goats and the Little Pink Pigs (with book)
   (DLM)

Classification, Opposites, Sequence (worksheets)
   (Ideal)

Familiar Sounds: Careers
   (DLM)

Gross Identification of Environmental Sounds
   (Perceptual Learning Systems)

Here are My Hands (with book)
   (DLM)

I Am Freedom's Child (with book)
   (DLM)

Ideal Tapes (vowels, consonants, blends, syllables, classification, opposites) (worksheets)
   (Ideal)

Initial and Final Consonants (worksheets)
   (Ideal)

Listening Skills Program, Primary Level 1 & 2
   (Science Research Associates)

Reading-Writing Readiness Reading Tapes (spiritmasters)
   (Ideal)

Syllable Rules and Accent Clues Structured Reading Tapes (spiritmasters)
   (Ideal)

Vowel Enrichment Tapes (spiritmasters)
   (Ideal)

Vowel Sounds (word wheels, worksheets)
   (Milton Bradley)

Walking Time Series, Sets 1 & 2 (storybook)
   (McGraw-Hill)

Word Building Reading Tapes (worksheets)
   (Ideal)

Word Function and Sentence Patterns (worksheets)
   (Ideal)

Workbooks and Reprint Masters

Auditory Discrimination, Beginning Sounds
  (Miliken)

Auditory Discrimination, Rhyming Sounds
  (Miliken)

Basic Word Study Skills for Middle Grades—Part 1: The Letters and Sounds in Words; and Part 2: Words and Their Parts
  (Ginn)

Big Book of Sounds
  (Pro-Ed)

Come and Hear
  (Follett)

Decoding for Reading
  (MacMillan)

English Syntax
  (Harcourt, Brace, Jovanavich)

Follow Me!
  (Lingui Systems)

Follow Me! Number 2
  (Lingui Systems)

Following Directions and Sequence (transparencies)
  (Milliken)

Learning to Think Series
  (Science Research Associates)

Lift Off Reading Cycles I, II, III
  (Science Research Associates)

Look and Listen
  (Ginn)

Match and Check Set
  (Scott Foresman)

New Phonics Skill Text Series
  (Charles E. Merrill)

Phonics in Fun Program
  (Modern Curriculum Press)

Reading Readiness Workbooks in Auditory Discrimination and Concepts
  (Follett)

Reading for Meaning Series
  (Houghton Mifflin)
Sound Foundations Practice Masters
  (DLM)
Sounds of Language Readers
  (Holt, Rinehart, and Winston)
Universal Workbooks in Phonics, Grades 1-5
  (Charles E. Merrill)

Addresses of the Publishers for the Listing of Commercially Produced Materials

Academic Press
525 B Street, Suite 1900
San Diego, California 92101-4495

Academic Therapy Publications
20 Commercial Boulevard
Novato, California 94949-6191

American Guidance Service
P.O. Box 99
Circle Pines, Minnesota 55014-1796

Ann Arbor Publishers
A Division of Academic Therapy
(See above)

Arcadia Press
37 Washington Square
New York, New York 10011

Bowmar/Noble Publishers
220 E. Danieldale Road
DeSota, Texas 75115

Creative Playthings
33 Loring Drive
Framingham, Massachusetts 01701

Thomas Y. Crowell
10 East 53rd Street
New York, New York 10022

Durrell Publishing, Inc.
Box 743
Kennebunkport, Maine 04046

Educational Activities, Inc.
P.O. Box 392
Freeport, New York 11520

Educational Development
200 West Bullard Avenue
Clovis, California 93612

Expression Company
Londondery, New Hampshire 03053

Eye-Gate House, Inc.
3333 Elston Avenue
Chicago, Illinois 60618

Follett Educational Corporation
2233 West Street
River Grove, Illinois 60171-1895

Ginn Press
160 Gould Street
Needham Heights, Massachusetts 02194

Harcourt, Brace and Company
525 B Street, Suite 1900
San Diego, California 92101

Holt, Rinehart and Winston
6277 Sea Harbor Drive
Orlando, Florida 32887

Houghton Mifflin Company
222 Berkeley Street
Boston, Massachusetts 02116-3764

Ideal Publishers
Box 140300
Nashville, Tennessee 37214

Kimbo Educational
P.O. Box 477
Long Branch, New Jersey 07740

Learning Research Associates, Inc.
P.O. Box 39
Roslyn Heights, New York 11577

LinguiSystems
Box 747
East Moline, Illinois 61244

Lippincott Company
220 East Danieldale Road
DeSota, Texas 75115

Little, Brown & Company
34 Beacon Street
Boston, Massachusetts 02108

Macmillan/McGraw Hill
P.O. Box 543
Blacklick, Ohio 43004-0544

McQueen Publishing Company
Box 198
Tiskilwa, Illinois 61368

Merrill Publishing Company
P.O. Box 543
Blacklick, Ohio 43004

Milliken Publishing Company
1100 Research Boulevard
St. Louis, Missouri 63132

Milton Bradley Company
443 Shaker Road
East Longmeadow, Massachusetts 01028

Modern Curriculum Press
4350 Equity Drive
Columbus, Ohio 43216

Norman Lathrop Enterprises
Box 198
Wooster, Ohio 44691

Prentice-Hall
200 Old Tappan
Old Tappan, New Jersey 07675

Pro-Ed
8700 Shoal Creek Boulevard
Austin, Texas 78757

Rand McNally & Company
Box 7600
Chicago, Illinois 60680

Random House
201 East 50th Street
New York, New York 10022

Scholastic, Incorporated
730 Broadway
New York, New York 10003

Science Research Associates
P.O. Box 543
Blacklick, Ohio 43004

Scott, Foresman/Harper Collins
1900 East Lake Avenue
Glenview, Illinois 60025

Society for Visual Education, Inc.
55 East Monroe, 34th Floor
Chicago, Illinois 60603-5710

Steck Vaughn
Box 26015
Austin, Texas 78755

Teachers College Press
Columbia University
1234 Amsterdam Avenue
New York, New York 10027

John Tracy Clinic
806 West Adams Boulevard
Los Angeles, California 90007

George Wahr Publishers
304½ South State Street
Ann Arbor, Michigan 48104

Western Publishing Company
1220 Mound Avenue
Racine, Wisconsin 53404

Worldbook-Childcraft International
Worldbook Book House
77 Mount Ephraim
Turnbridge Wells, Kent
England TN4 8A2

ABOUT THE AUTHOR: Pamela Gillet, Ph.D., has been Superintendent of the Northwest Surburban Special Education Organization in Mt. Prospect, Illinois, since 1979 and has been a college instructor for more than 20 years. She previously was a teacher in both regular and special education classrooms for 10 years. Her published works include: *Career Education for LD Students* and *Of Work and Worth,* as well as articles in professional journals and publications such as "Teaching Exceptional Children" and "Instructor" magazines.